HAL•LEONARD®

BASS
PLAY-ALONG

IRON MAIDEN

AUDIO
ACCESS
INCLUDED

Cover photo: John McMurtrie, Iron Maiden LLP

PLAYBACK+
Speed • Pitch • Balance • Loop

To access audio visit:
www.halleonard.com/mylibrary
Enter Code
3750-2544-9071-0884

ISBN 978-1-5400-2974-4

HAL•LEONARD®

Visit Hal Leonard Online at
www.halleonard.com

Contact us:
Hal Leonard
7777 West Bluemound Road
Milwaukee, WI 53213
Email: info@halleonard.com

In Europe, contact:
Hal Leonard Europe Limited
42 Wigmore Street
Marylebone, London, W1U 2RN
Email: info@halleonardeurope.com

In Australia, contact:
Hal Leonard Australia Pty. Ltd.
4 Lentara Court
Cheltenham, Victoria, 3192 Australia
Email: info@halleonard.com.au

BASS NOTATION LEGEND

Bass music can be notated two different ways: on a *musical staff*, and in *tablature*.

THE MUSICAL STAFF shows pitches and rhythms and is divided by bar lines into measures. Pitches are named after the first seven letters of the alphabet.

TABLATURE graphically represents the bass fingerboard. Each horizontal line represents a string, and each number represents a fret.

Notes:

3rd string, open   2nd string, 2nd fret   1st & 2nd strings open, played together

HAMMER-ON: Strike the first (lower) note with one finger, then sound the higher note (on the same string) with another finger by fretting it without picking.

PULL-OFF: Place both fingers on the notes to be sounded. Strike the first note and without picking, pull the finger off to sound the second (lower) note.

LEGATO SLIDE: Strike the first note and then slide the same fret-hand finger up or down to the second note. The second note is not struck.

SHIFT SLIDE: Same as legato slide, except the second note is struck.

TRILL: Very rapidly alternate between the notes indicated by continuously hammering on and pulling off.

TREMOLO PICKING: The note is picked as rapidly and continuously as possible.

VIBRATO: The string is vibrated by rapidly bending and releasing the note with the fretting hand.

SHAKE: Using one finger, rapidly alternate between two notes on one string by sliding either a half-step above or below.

NATURAL HARMONIC: Strike the note while the fret hand lightly touches the string directly over the fret indicated.

MUFFLED STRINGS: A percussive sound is produced by laying the fret hand across the string(s) without depressing them and striking them with the pick hand.

BEND: Strike the note and bend up the interval shown.

BEND AND RELEASE: Strike the note and bend up as indicated, then release back to the original note. Only the first note is struck.

RIGHT-HAND TAP: Hammer ("tap") the fret indicated with the "pick-hand" index or middle finger and pull off to the note fretted by the fret hand.

LEFT-HAND TAP: Hammer ("tap") the fret indicated with the "fret-hand" index or middle finger.

SLAP: Strike ("slap") string with right-hand thumb.

POP: Snap ("pop") string with right-hand index or middle finger.

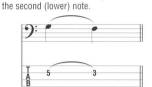

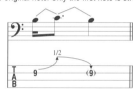

Additional Musical Definitions

(accent)	• Accentuate note (play it louder).	
(accent)	• Accentuate note with great intensity.	
(staccato)	• Play the note short.	
⊓	• Downstroke	
V	• Upstroke	

D.S. al Coda   • Go back to the sign (%), then play until the measure marked "*To Coda*," then skip to the section labelled "*Coda*."

D.C. al Fine   • Go back to the beginning of the song and play until the measure marked "*Fine*" (end).

Bass Fig.   • Label used to recall a recurring pattern.

Fill   • Label used to identify a brief melodic figure which is to be inserted into the arrangement.

tacet   • Instrument is silent (drops out).

• Repeat measures between signs.

• When a repeated section has different endings, play the first ending only the first time and the second ending only the second time.

NOTE: Tablature numbers in parentheses mean:
1. The note is being sustained over a system (note in standard notation is tied), or
2. The note is sustained, but a new articulation (such as a hammer-on, pull-off, slide or vibrato) begins.

Aces High

Words and Music by Steve Harris

Intro

Moderately fast Rock ♩ = 160

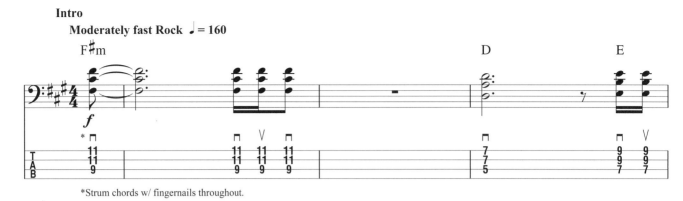

*Strum chords w/ fingernails throughout.

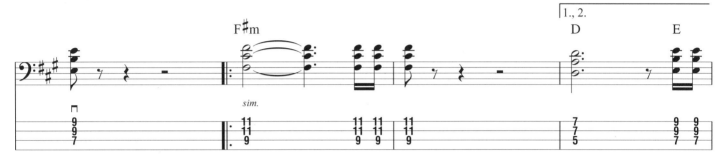

Faster ♩ = 252

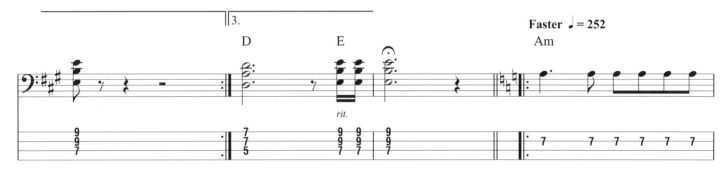

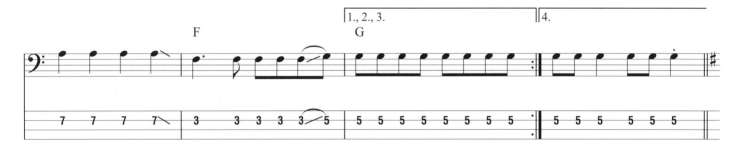

Verse

1. There goes ___ the si - ren ___ that warns of ___ the air raid, ___
2. *See additional lyrics*

move all ___ the wheel - blocks, ___ there's no time ___ to waste.

Gath - er - - - ing speed as ___ we head down ___ the run - way, ___

got - ta ___ get air - borne ___ be - fore it's ___ too late.

Pre-Chorus

Em

1., 2. Run - nin',   scramb - lin',   fly - in'.
3., 4. Roll - in',   turn - in',   div - in'.

Roll - in', turn - in', div - in'. Go - ing in a - gain.

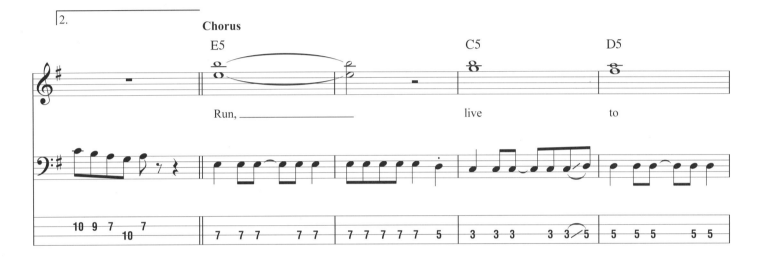

Run, live to

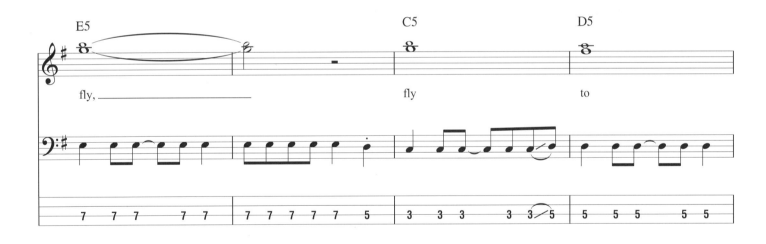

fly, fly to

live, do or

9

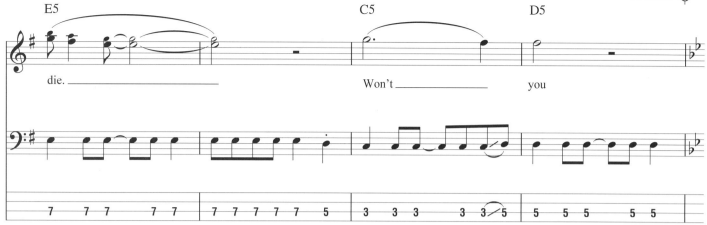

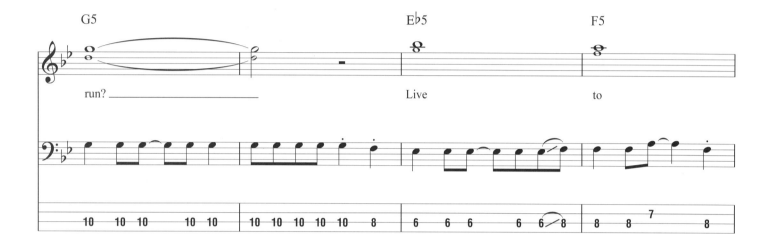

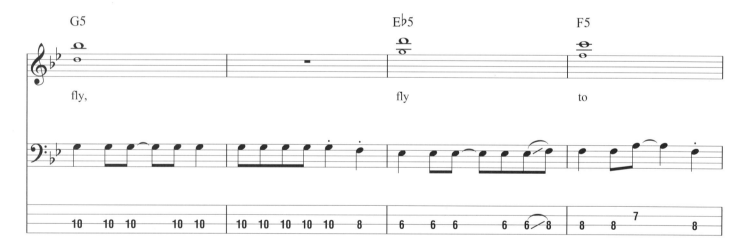

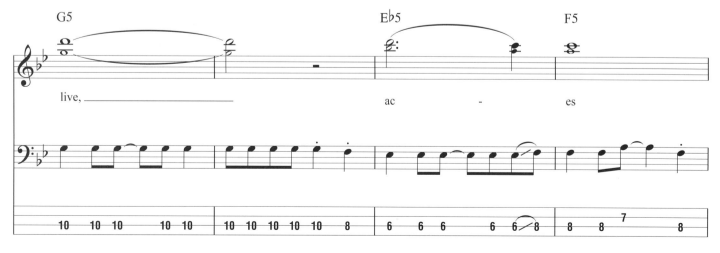

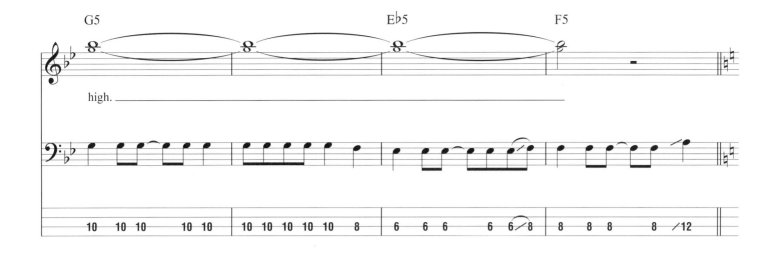

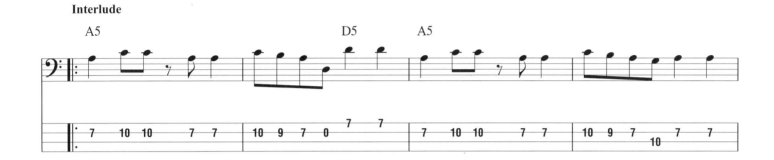

Interlude

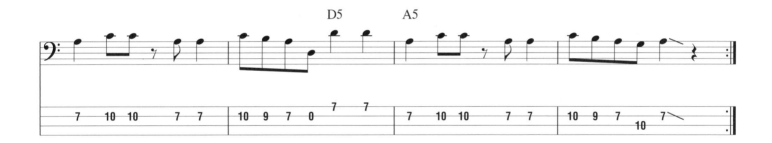

Guitar Solo

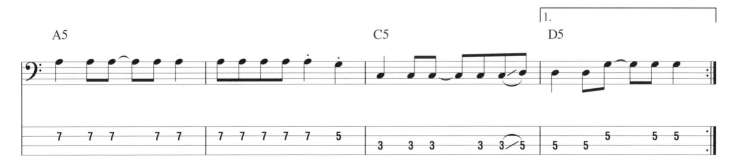

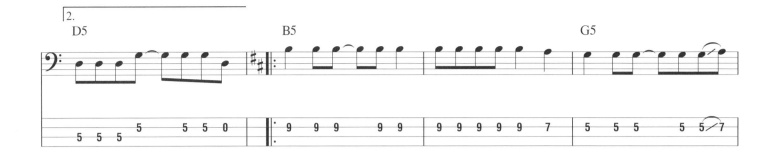

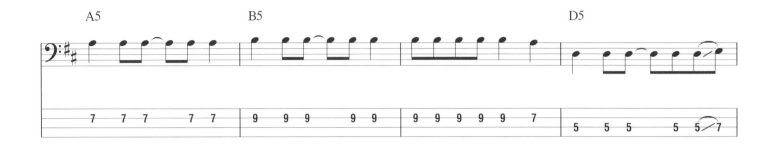

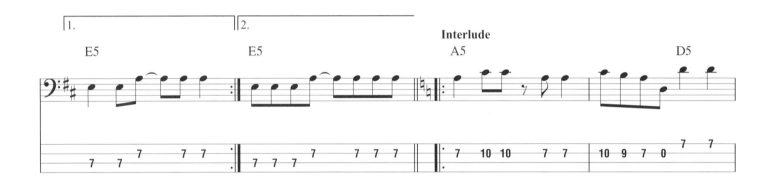

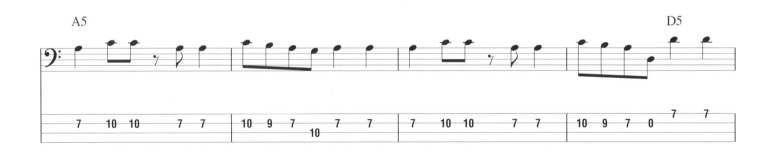

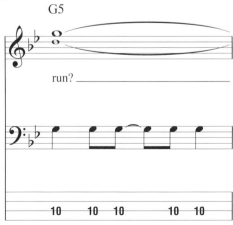

Live to fly,

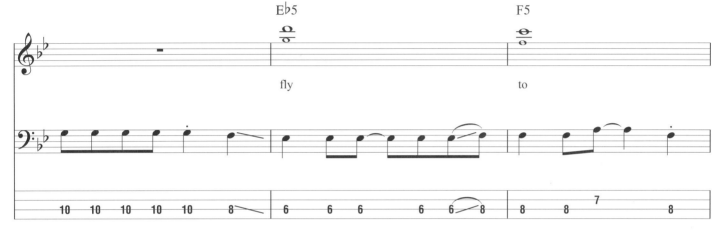

fly to

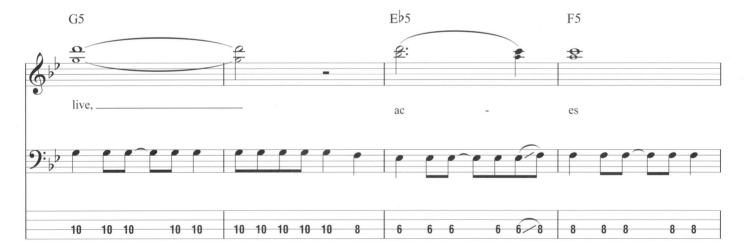

live, ac - es

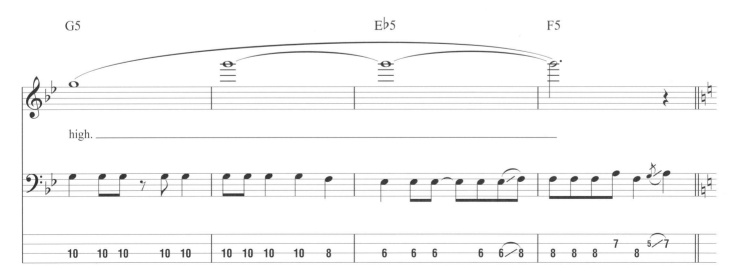

high.

Outro

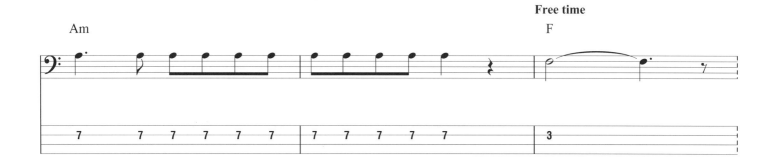

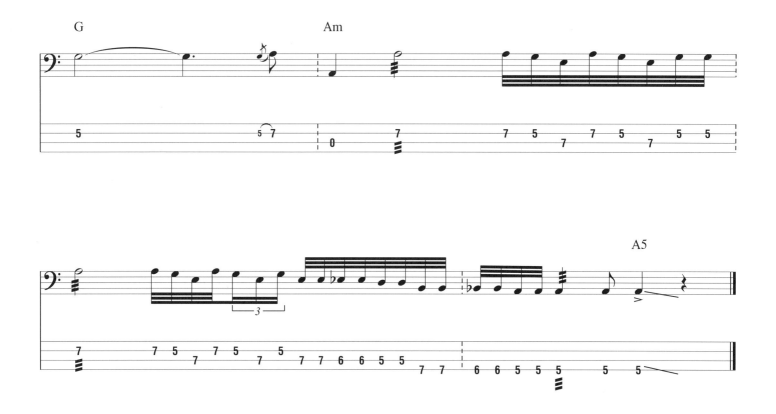

Additional Lyrics

2. Move in to fire at the mainstream of bombers.
Let off a sharp burst and then turn away.
Roll over, spin 'round and come in behind them.
Move to their blindsides and firing again.
Bandits at eight o'clock move in behind us,
Ten Me-109s out of the sun.
Ascending and turning our Spitfires to face them,
Heading straight for them, I press down my guns.

The Number of the Beast

Words and Music by Steve Harris

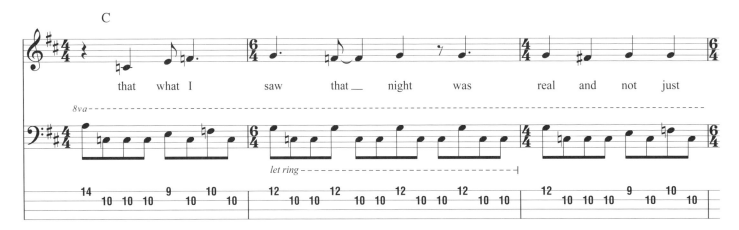

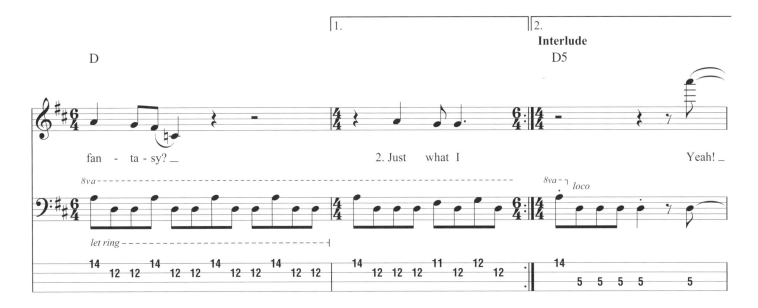

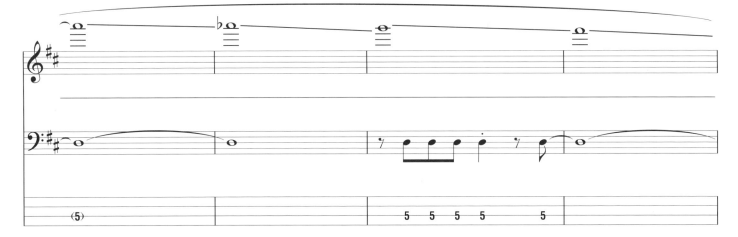

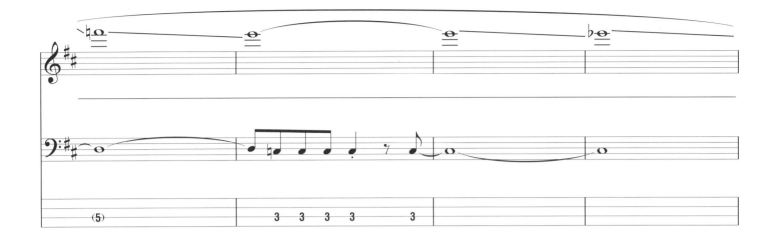

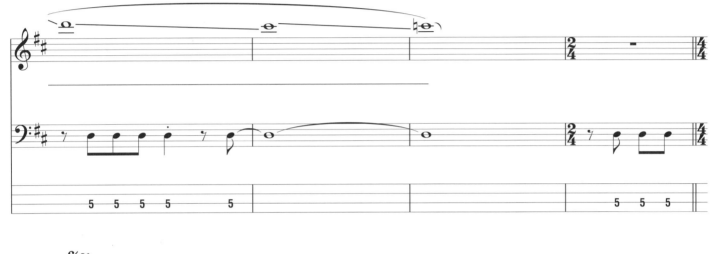

3. Night was __ black, was no use hold - ing __ back 'cause I just
4., 5. *See additional lyrics*

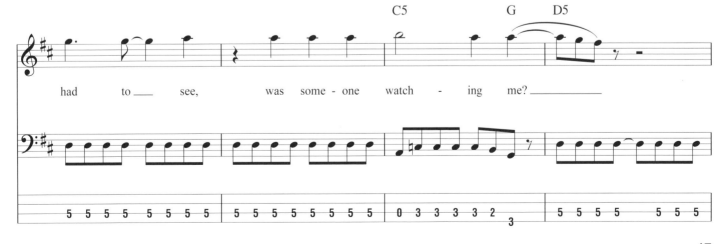

had to __ see, was some - one watch - ing me? ___

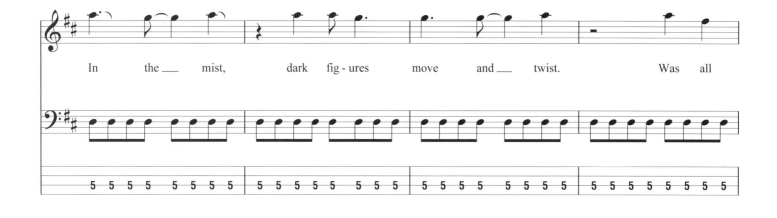

In the ___ mist, dark fig-ures move and ___ twist. Was all

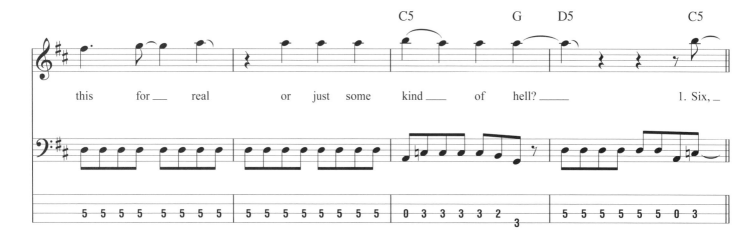

this for ___ real or just some kind ___ of hell? _____ 1. Six, ___

Chorus

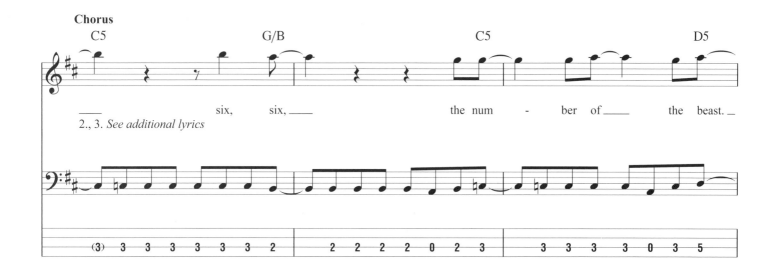

___ six, six, ___ the num - ber of ___ the beast. ___

2., 3. *See additional lyrics*

To Coda ⊕

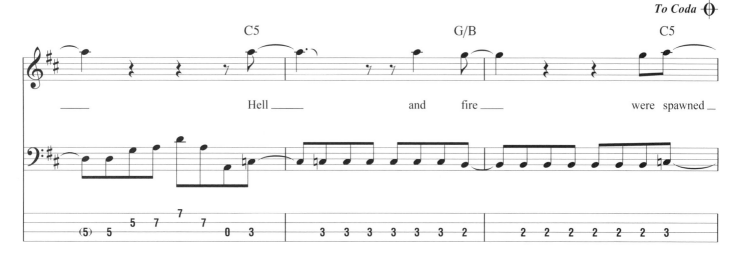

___ Hell ___ and fire ___ were spawned __

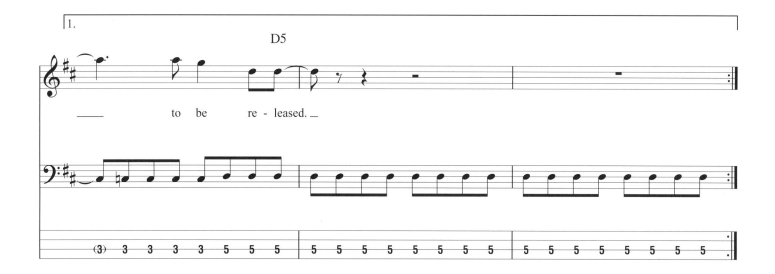

to be re - leased.

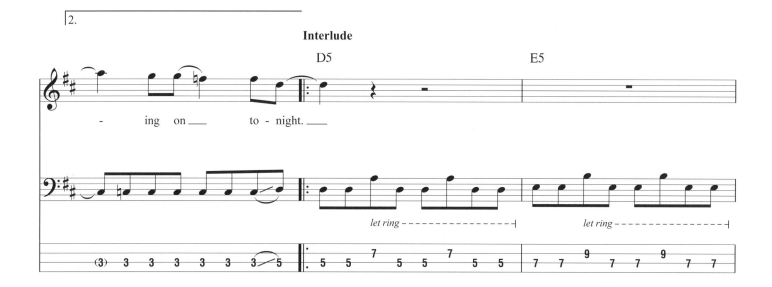

Interlude

- ing on to - night.

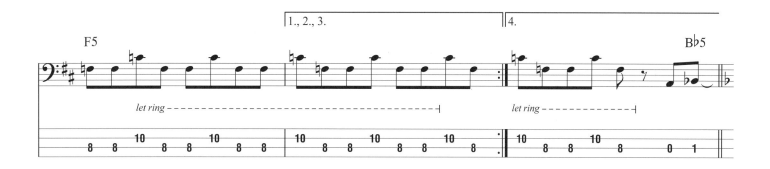

Guitar Solo

Play 3 times

Interlude

Guitar Solo

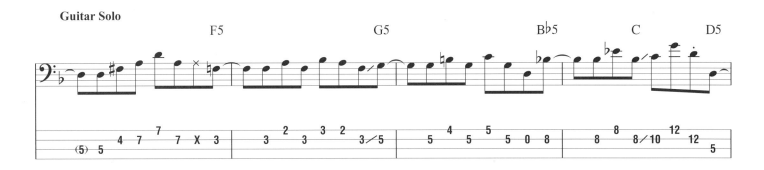

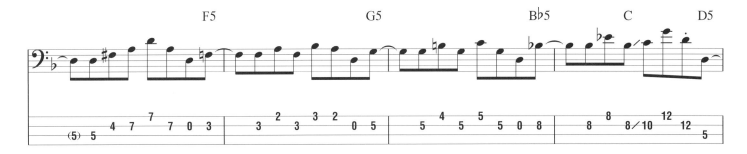

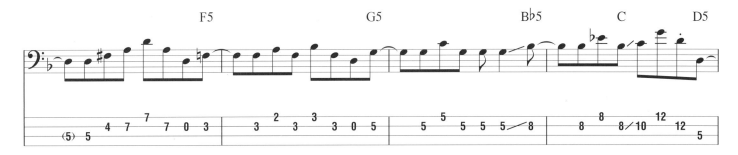

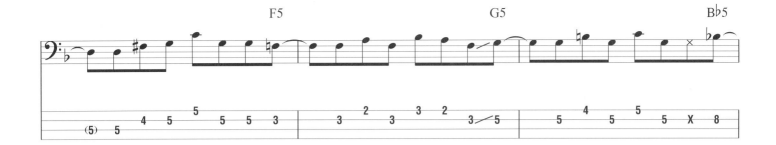

Interlude

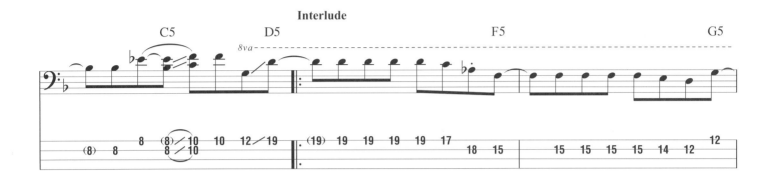

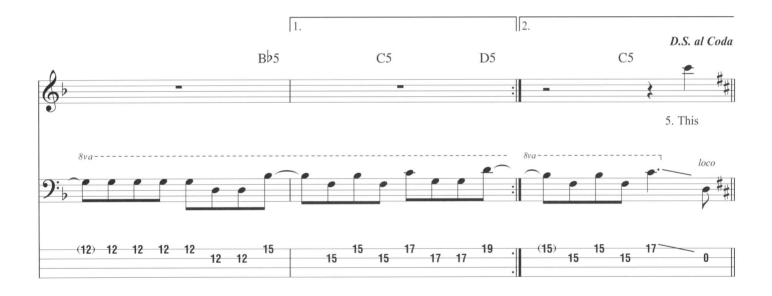

5. This

for   you and   me. __

Verse

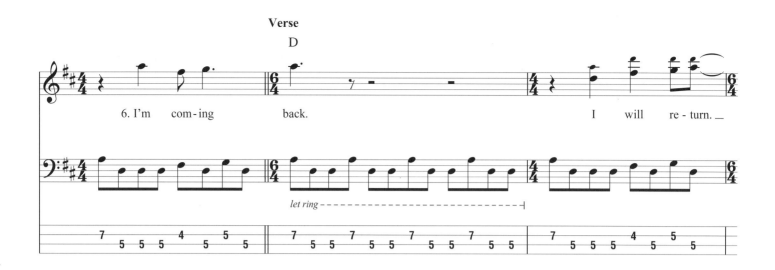

6. I'm com-ing back.   I will re - turn.

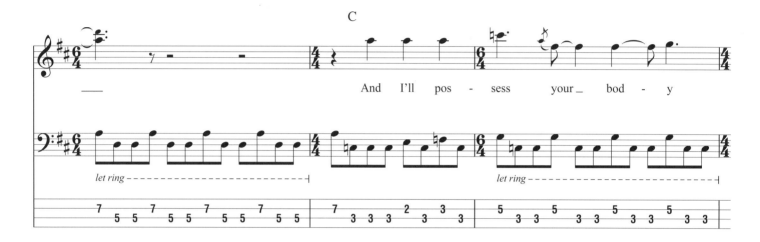

And I'll pos - sess your bod - y

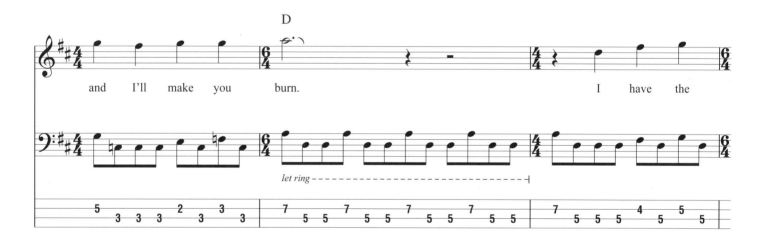

and I'll make you burn.   I have the

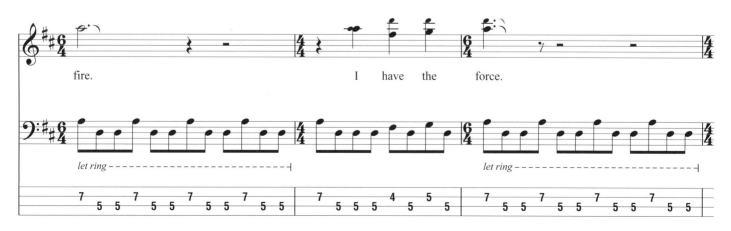

fire.   I have the force.

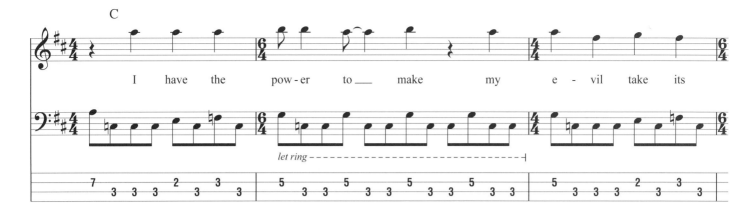

Outro

Additional Lyrics

2. Just what I saw in my old dreams,
Were they reflections of my warped mind staring back at me?
'Cause in my dreams it's always there,
The evil face that twists my mind and brings me to despair.

4. Torches blazed and sacred chants were praised
As they start to cry, hands held to the sky.
In the night, the fires are burning bright.
The ritual has begun. Satan's work is done.

Chorus 2. Six, six, six, the number of the beast.
Sacrifice is going on tonight.

5. This can't go on, I must inform the law.
Can they still be real or just some crazy dream?
But I feel drawn towards the chanting hordes,
Seem to mesmerize, can't avoid their eyes.

Chorus 3. Six, six, six, the number of the beast.
Six, six, six, the one for you and me.

Flight of Icarus

Words and Music by Bruce Dickinson and Adrian Smith

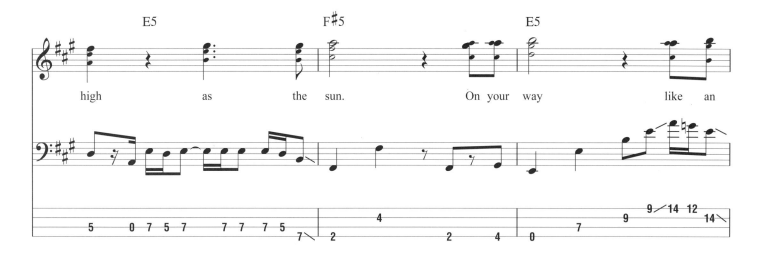

high   as   the sun.   On your way   like an

To Coda 2 ⊕

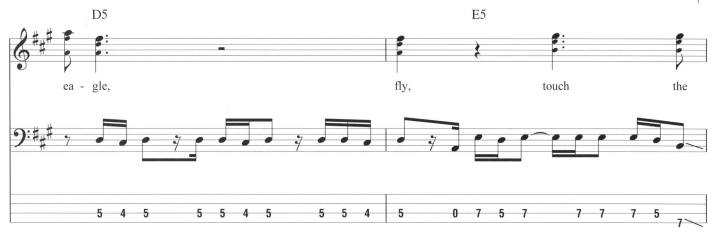

ea - gle,   fly,   touch   the

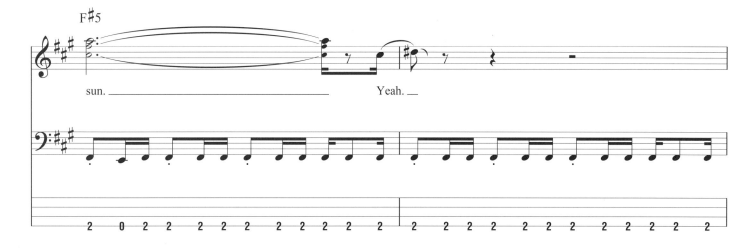

sun. _____   Yeah. _____

D.S. al Coda 1

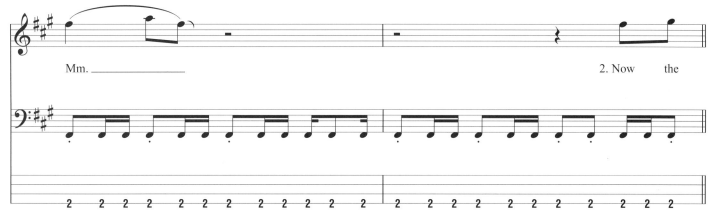

Mm. _____   2. Now   the

⊕ Coda 1

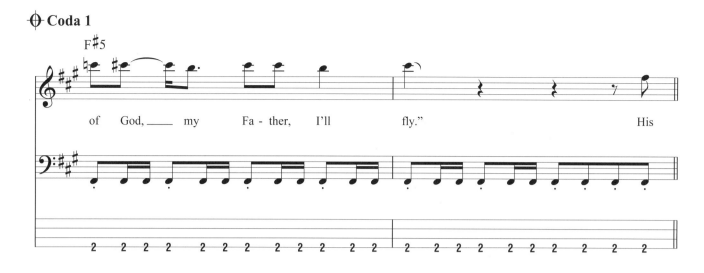

of God, ____ my Fa - ther, I'll fly." His

Pre-Chorus

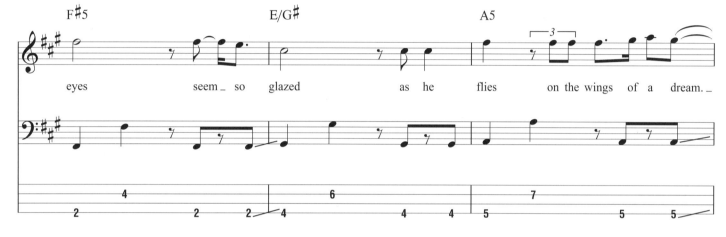

eyes seem _ so glazed as he flies on the wings of a dream. _

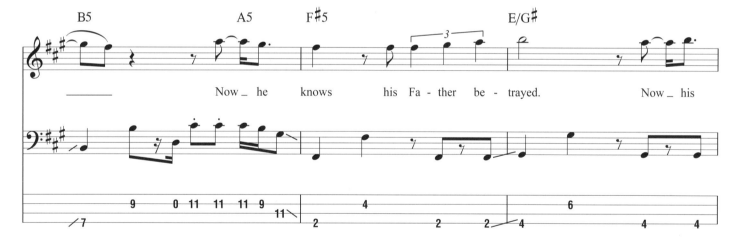

____ Now _ he knows his Fa - ther be - trayed. Now _ his

D.S.S. al Coda 2

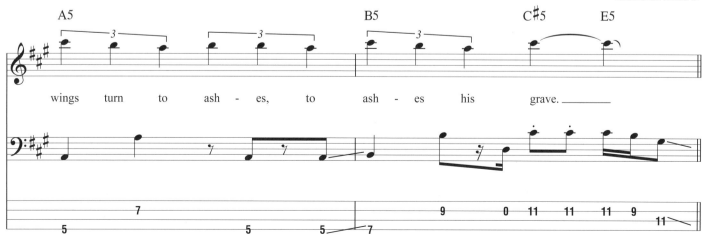

wings turn to ash - es, to ash - es his grave. _____

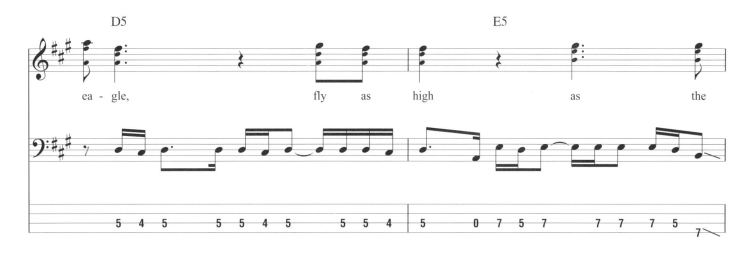

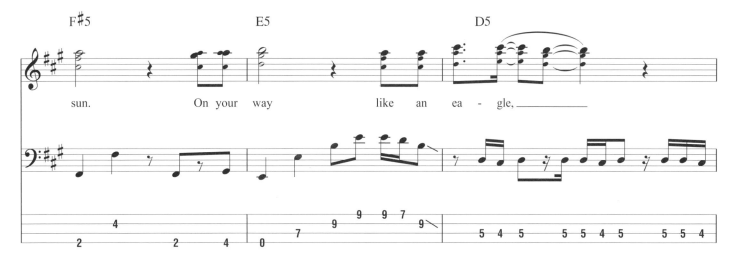

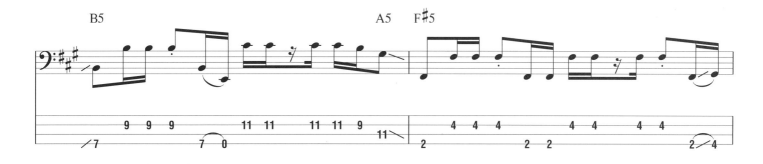

Fly as high as the

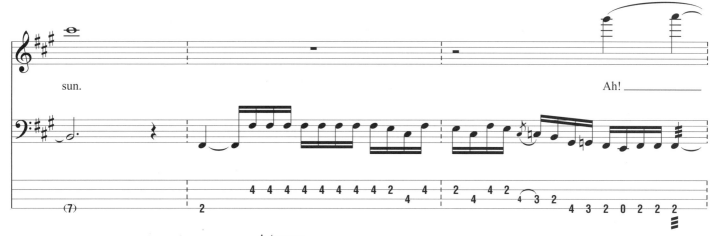

sun.

Ah! _____

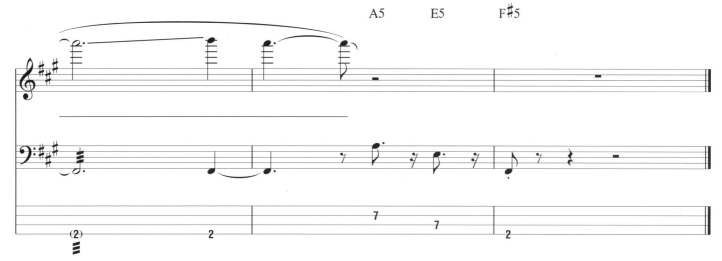

Additional Lyrics

2. Now the crowd breaks and a young boy appears.
Looks the old man in the eye,
As he spreads his wings and shouts at the crowd,
"In the name of God, my Father, I'll fly."

Run to the Hills

Words and Music by Steve Harris

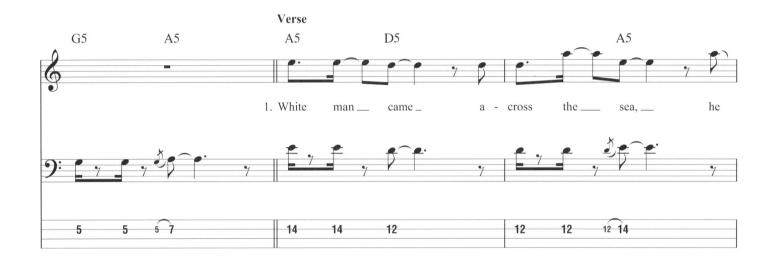

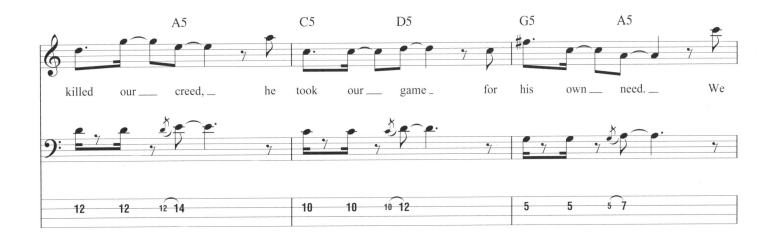

killed our __ creed, __ he took our __ game __ for his own __ need. __ We

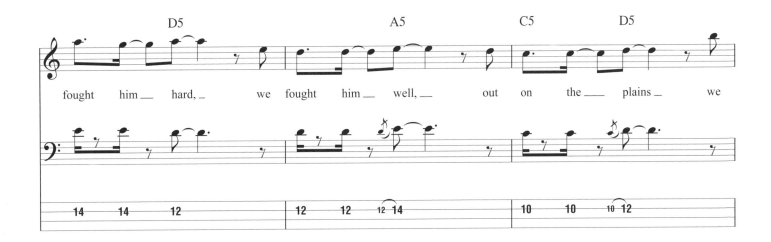

fought him __ hard, __ we fought him __ well, __ out on the __ plains __ we

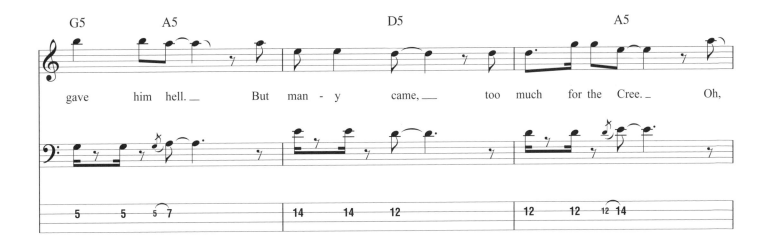

gave him hell. __ But man - y came, __ too much for the Cree. __ Oh,

will we __ ev - er _____ be set __ free? __

Interlude

Faster ♩ = 180

Verse

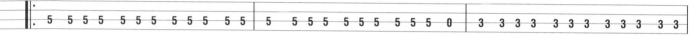

2. Rid - ing through dust clouds and bar - ren wastes, __ gal - lop - ing hard on the
3. *See additional lyrics*

plains. __ Chas - ing the red - skins back to their holes,

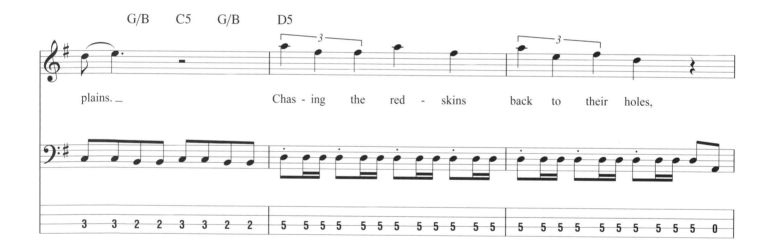

fight - ing them at their own game. __ Mur - der for free - dom, the

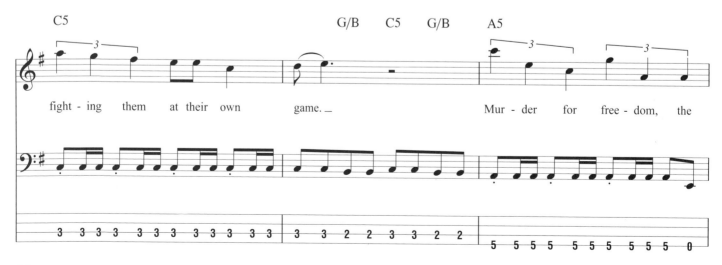

34

Interlude

Yeah. _____

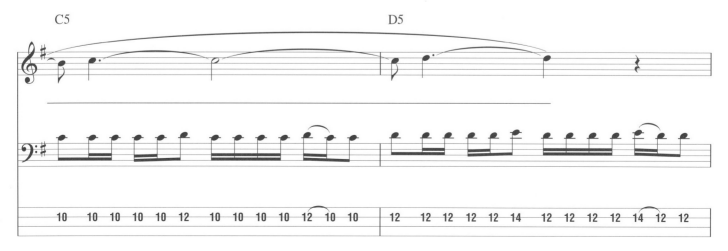

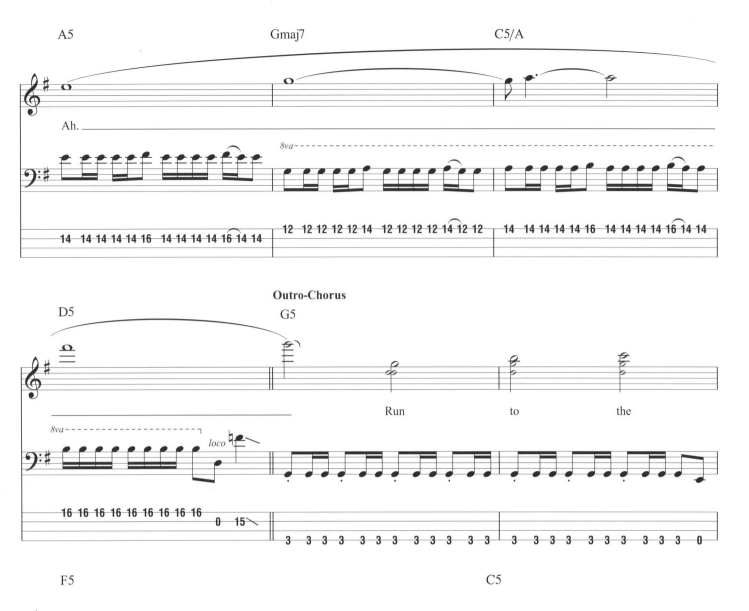

Outro-Chorus

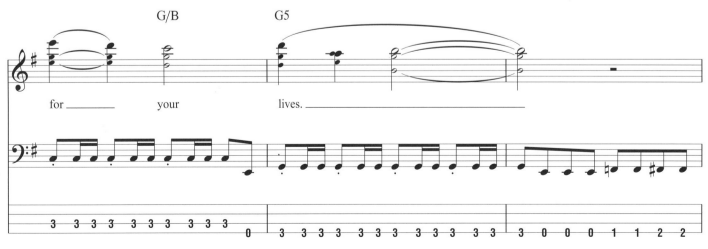

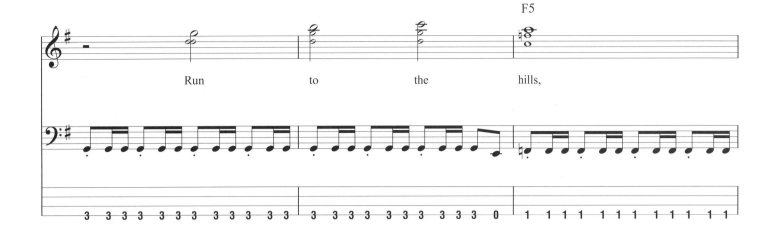

Run   to   the   hills,

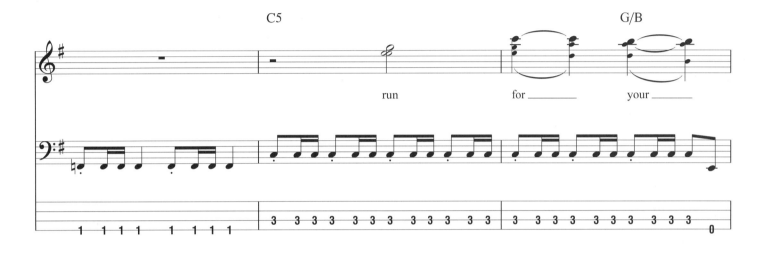

run   for _____   your _____

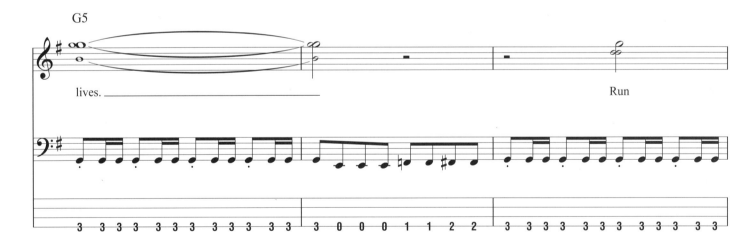

lives. _____   Run

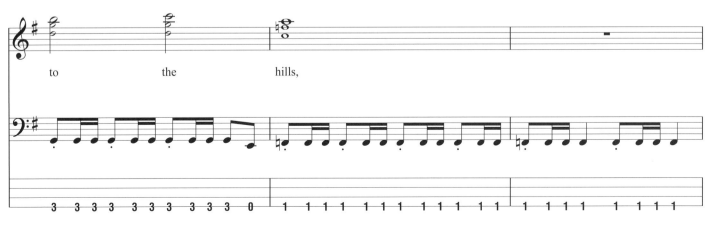

to   the   hills,

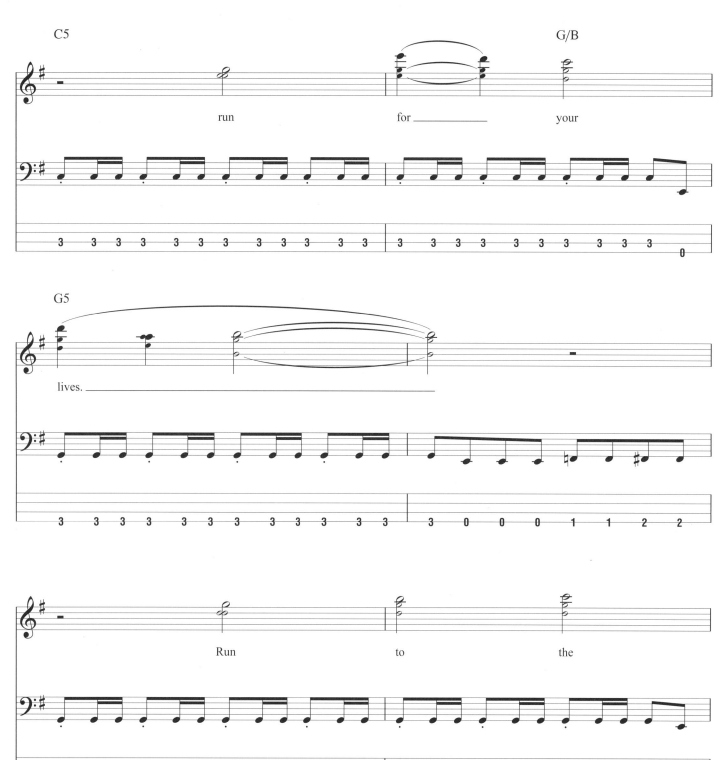

run   for _____ your

lives. _____

Run   to   the

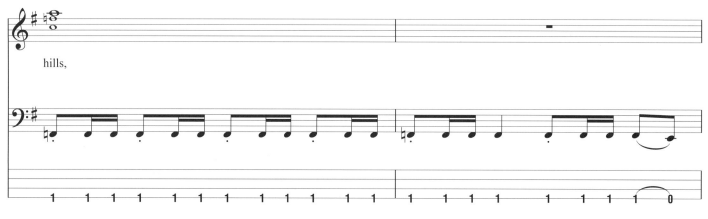

hills,

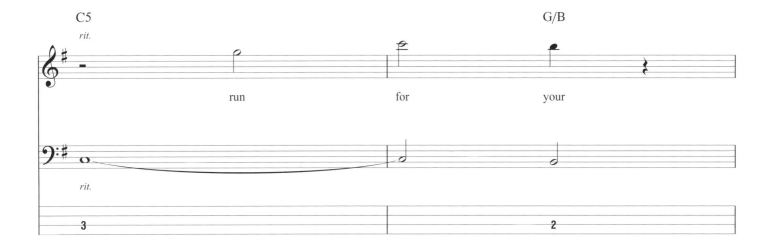

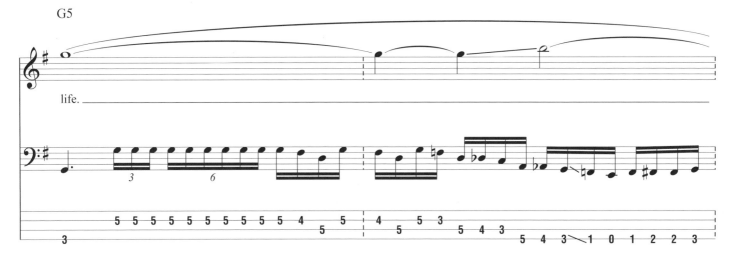

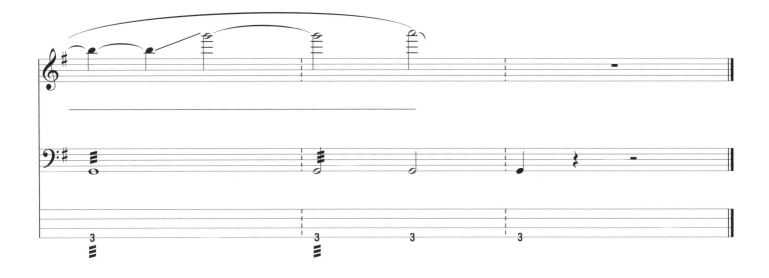

Additional Lyrics

3. Soldier blue in the barren wastes,
Hunting and killing's a game.
Raping the women and wasting the men;
The only good injuns are tame.
Selling them whiskey and taking their gold,
Enslaving the young and destroying the old.

Running Free

Words and Music by Steve Harris and Paul Andrews

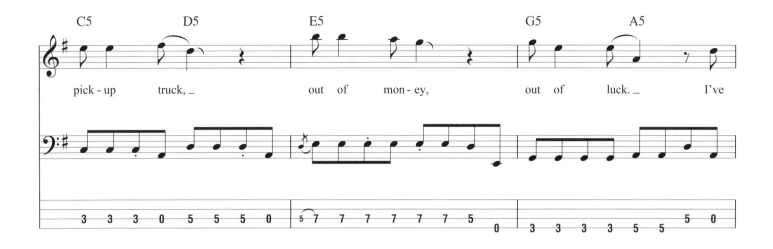

pick - up truck, _ out of mon - ey, out of luck. _ I've

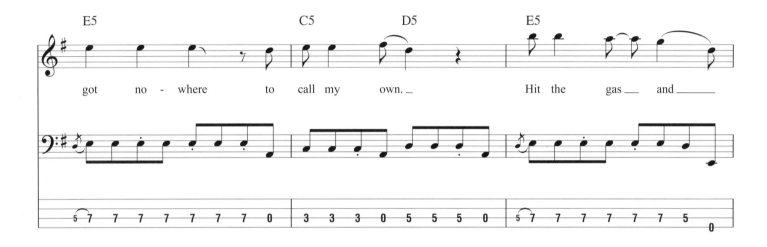

got no - where to call my own. _ Hit the gas __ and _____

% Chorus

here I go. _ I'm run - nin' free, ___ yeah. _

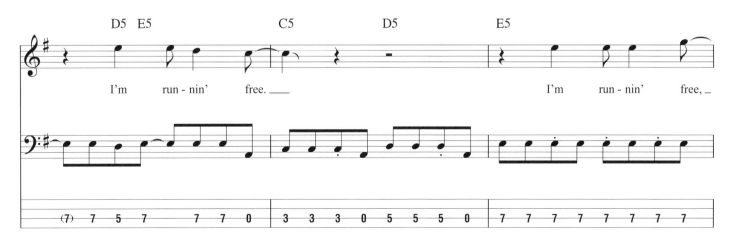

I'm run - nin' free. ___ I'm run - nin' free, _

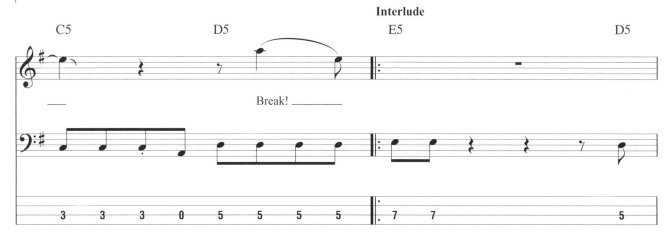

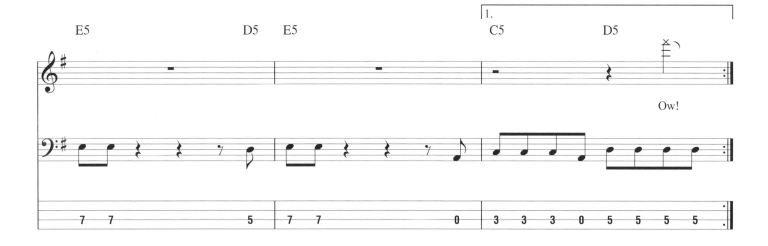

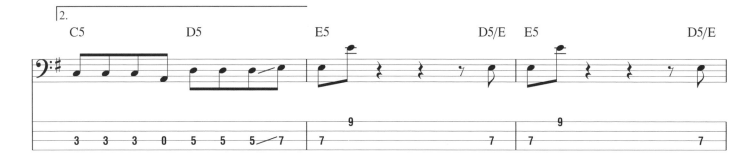

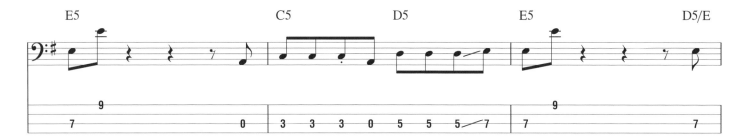

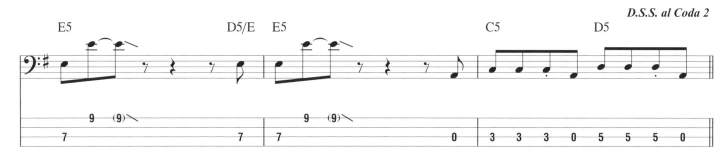

Coda 2

Oo, yeah. Run - nin', I'm run - nin', I'm

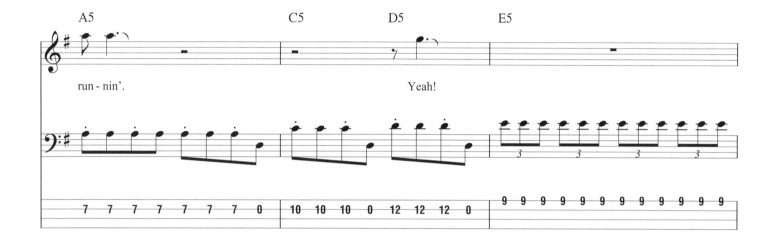

run - nin'. Yeah!

Ow, ow! Ow, ow! _____

Additional Lyrics

2. I spent the night in L.A. jail
   And listened to the sirens wail.
   But they ain't got a thing on me.
   I'm runnin' wild, I'm runnin' free.

3. Pulled her at the Bottle Top,
   A whiskey, dancing, disco hop.
   Now all the boys are after me,
   And that's the way it's gonna be, hey.

The Trooper

Words and Music by Steve Harris

Intro
Moderately fast ♩ = 160

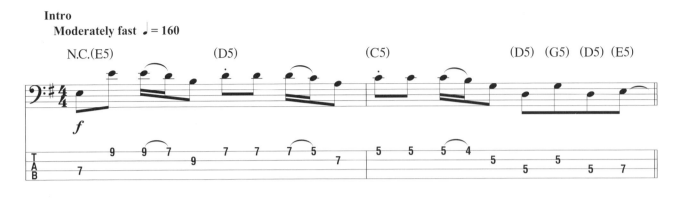

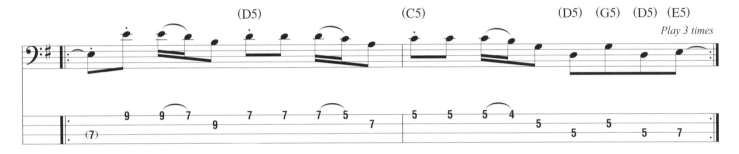

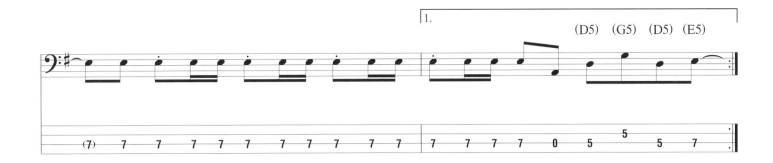

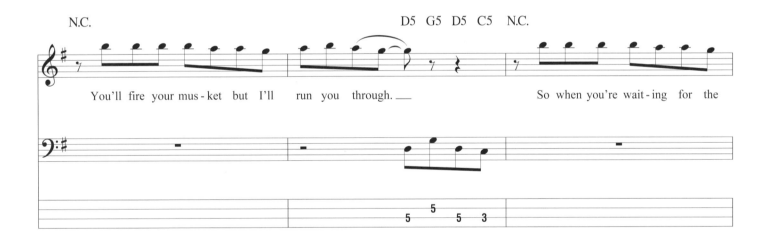

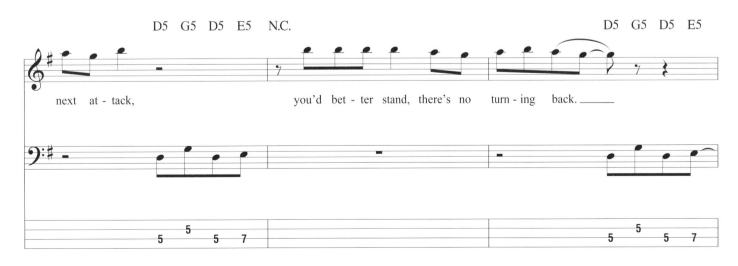

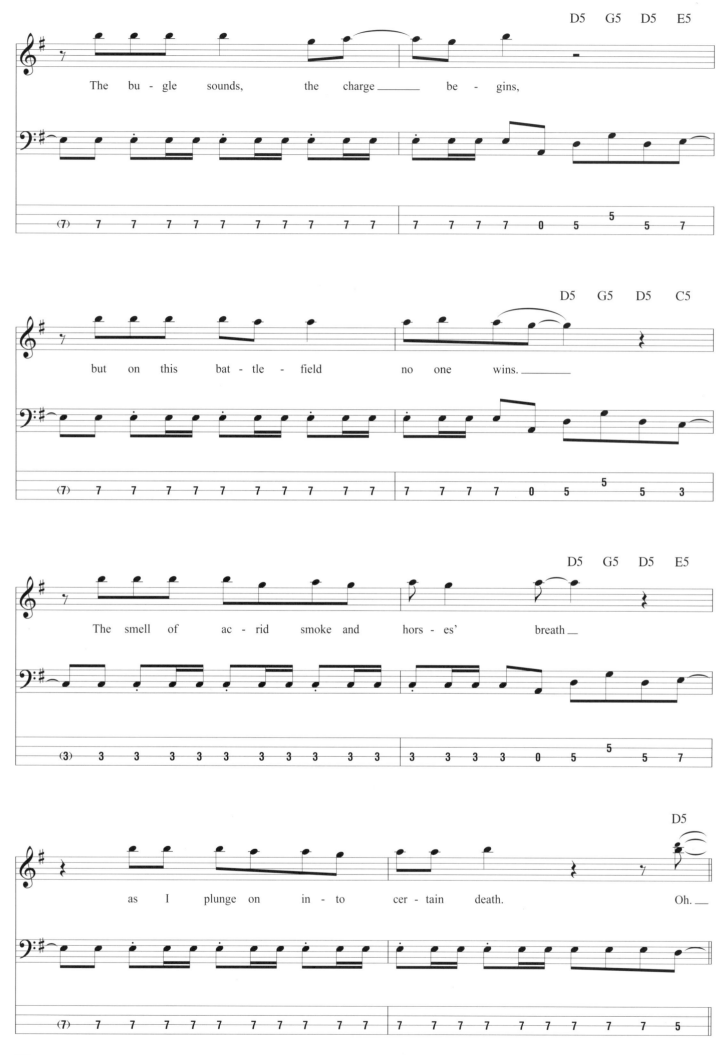

Chorus

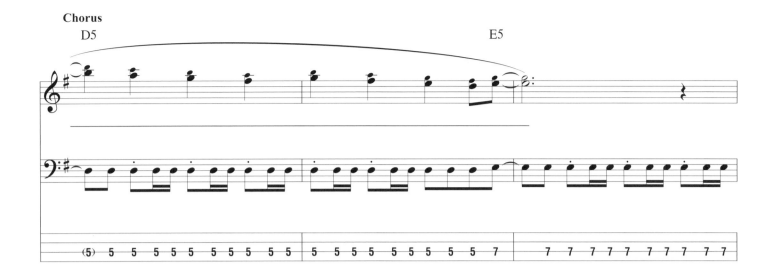

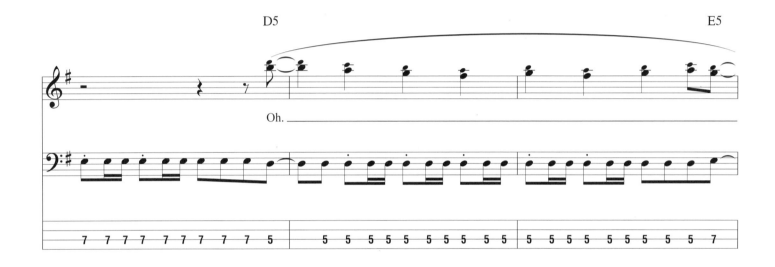

𝄉 Interlude

Verse

2. The horse, he sweats with fear, we break to run. _____ The might‑y roar _ of the
3. *See additional lyrics*

Rus‑sian guns. _____ And as we race to‑wards the hu‑man wall,

the screams of pain as my com‑rades fall. We hur‑dle bod‑ies that lay

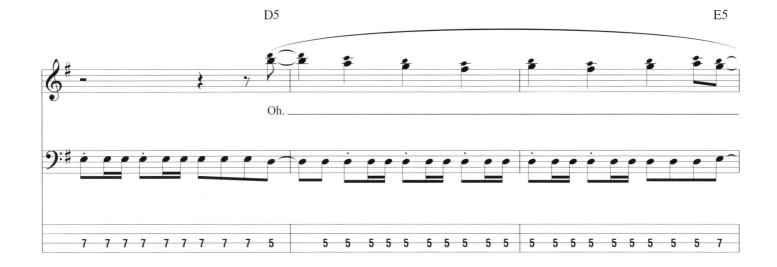

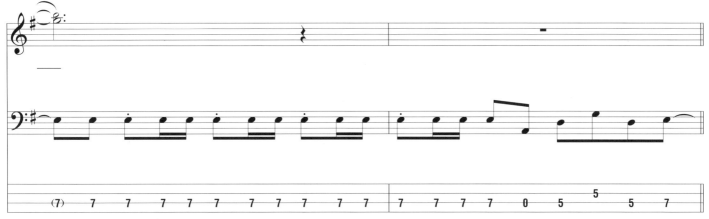

Guitar Solo

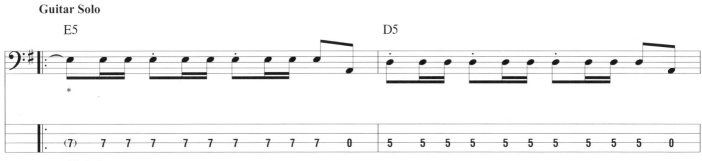

*Omit tie on repeats.

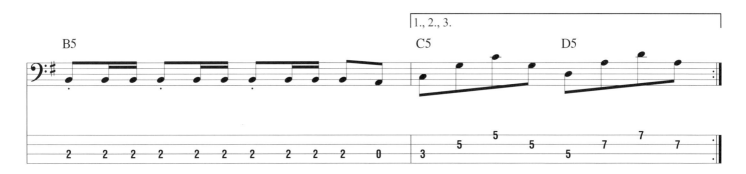

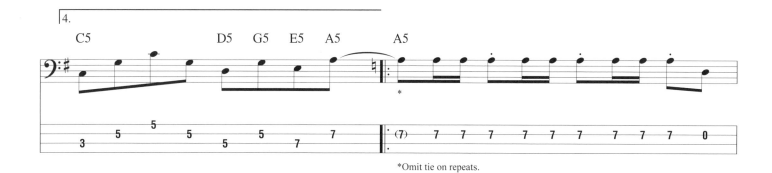

*Omit tie on repeats.

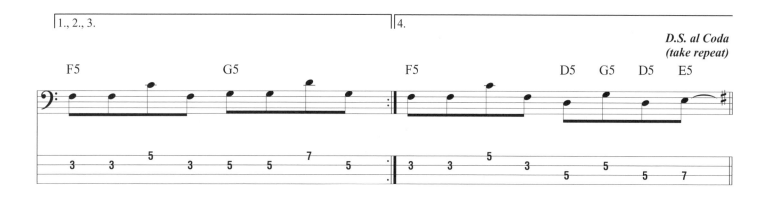

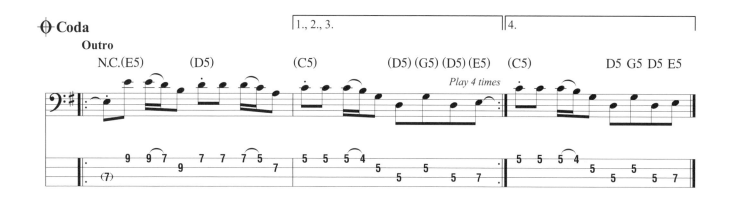

Additional Lyrics

3. We get so close, near enough to fight,
   When a Russian gets me in his sights.
   He pulls the trigger and I feel the blow,
   A burst of rounds takes my horse below.
   And as I lay there gazing at the sky,
   My body's numb and my throat is dry.
   And as I lay forgotten and alone,
   Without a tear I draw my parting groan.

Two Minutes to Midnight

Words and Music by Bruce Dickinson and Adrian Smith

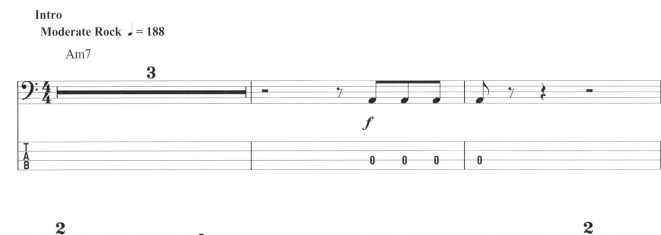

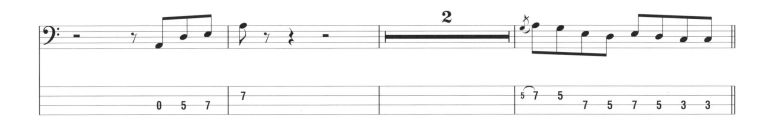

Verse

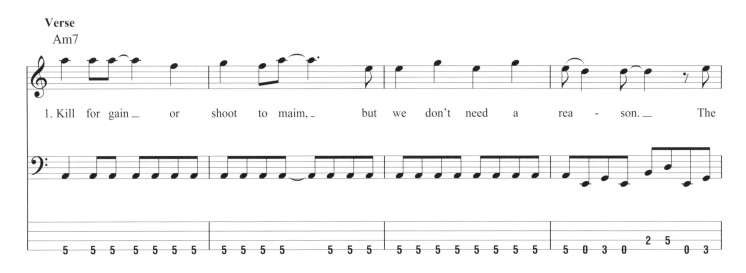

1. Kill for gain __ or shoot to maim, __ but we don't need a rea - son. __ The

Gold - en Goose _ is on the loose _ and nev - er out _ of sea - son. _

D5

Black - ened pride _ still burns in - side this shell of blood - y trea - son.

Am7   D5

Here's my gun for a bar - rel of fun, _ for the love of liv - ing death. _ The

𝄋 Pre-Chorus
Half-time feel

Am   F/A   G/A   Am7

kill - er's _ breed _ or the de - mon's seed. The

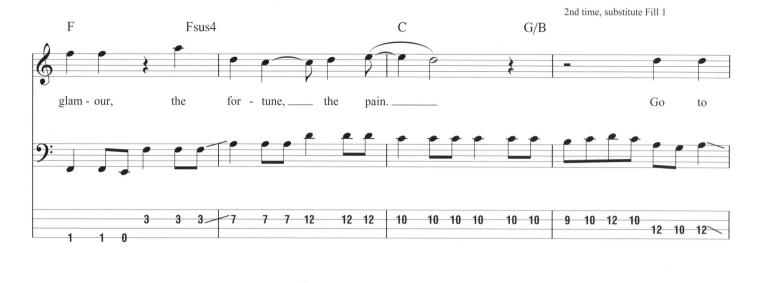

2nd time, substitute Fill 1

glam - our, the for - tune, ___ the pain. ___ Go to

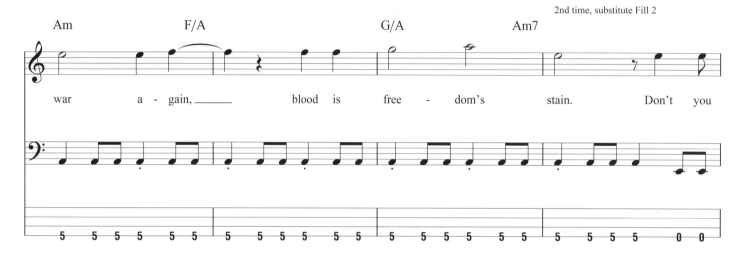

2nd time, substitute Fill 2

war a - gain, ___ blood is free - dom's stain. Don't you

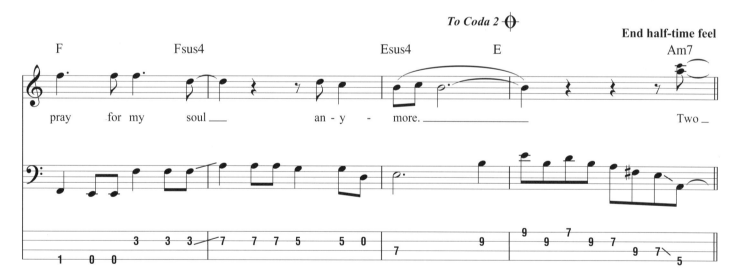

To Coda 2

End half-time feel

pray for my soul ___ an - y - more. ___ Two ___

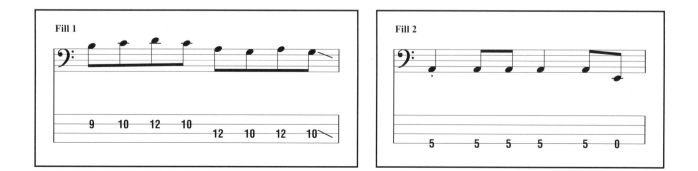

Chorus

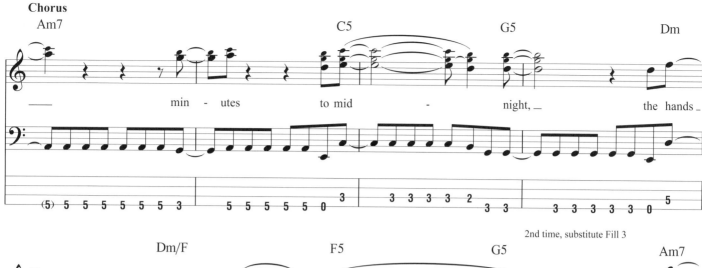

min - utes to mid - night, __ the hands __

2nd time, substitute Fill 3

that threat - en _____ doom. _____ Two _

min - utes to mid - night, __ to kill _

To Coda 1 ⊕

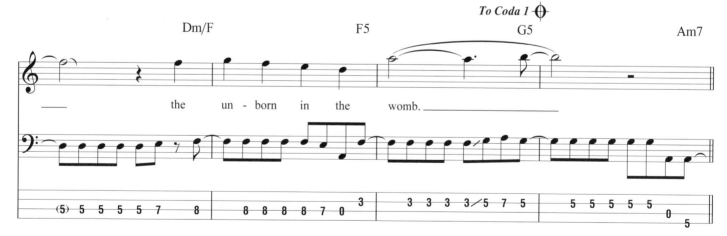

the un - born in the womb. _____

Fill 3

Interlude

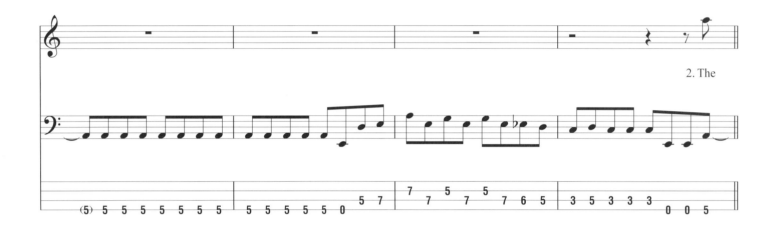

2. The

Verse

blind men shout, let the crea - tures out, ___ we'll show the un - be - liev - ers. ___ The

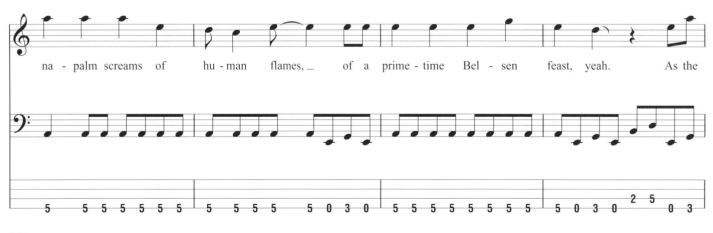

na - palm screams of hu - man flames, ___ of a prime - time Bel - sen feast, yeah. As the

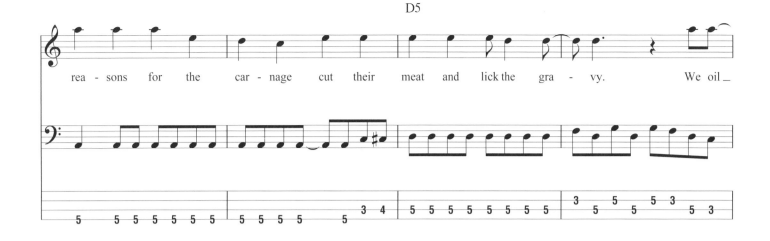

rea - sons for the car - nage cut their meat and lick the gra - vy. We oil __

D5

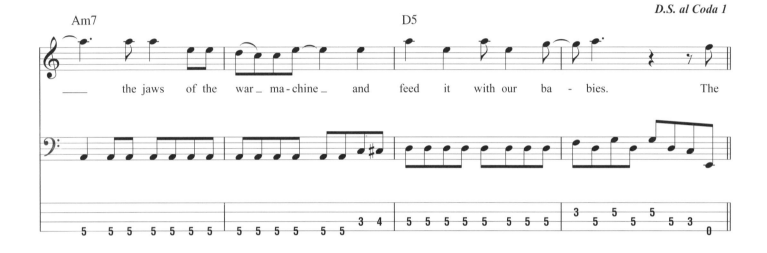

D.S. al Coda 1

Am7   D5

__ the jaws of the war __ ma - chine __ and feed it with our ba - bies. The

Coda 1

Guitar Solo

A5   F5   C/E   Dadd4

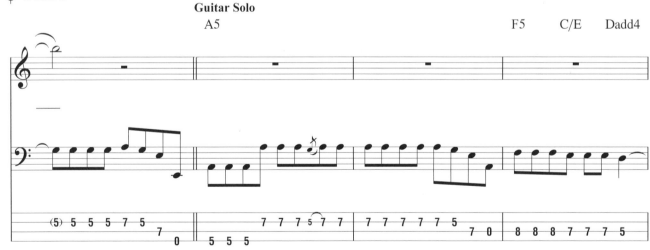

A5   E5/A   G5/A   F5   C/E   D5

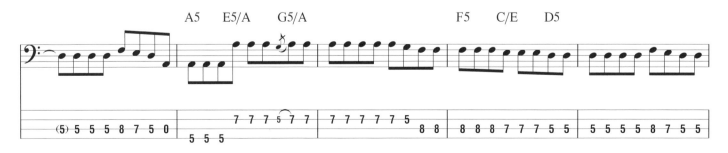

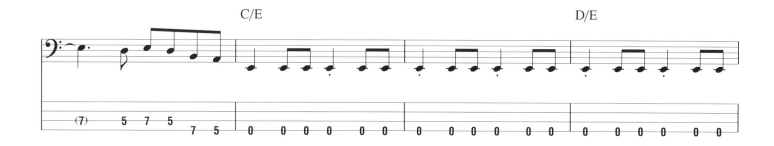

C/E   D/E

Em

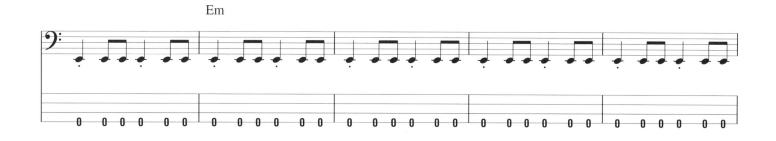

C/E   D5/E

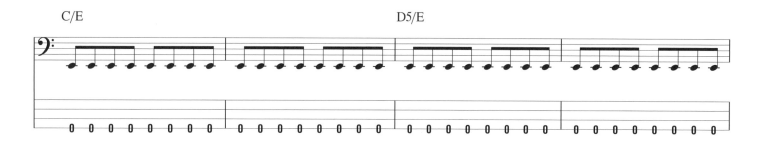

End half-time feel

E5

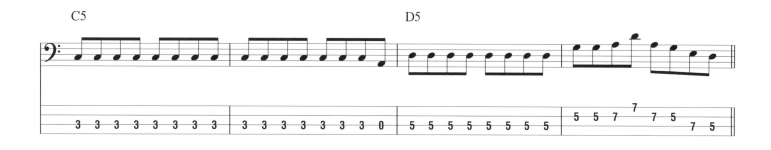

C5   D5

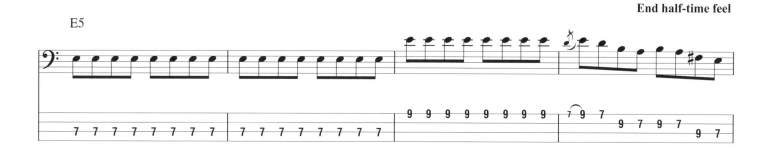

Interlude

Am7

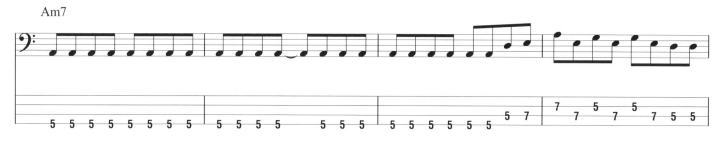

Verse

Am7

bod-y bags __ and lit-tle rags __ of chil-dren torn in two. And the

jel-lied brains __ of those who re-main __ to put the fin-ger right on you. __ As the

D5

mad men play on words __ and make us all __ dance __ to their song. To the

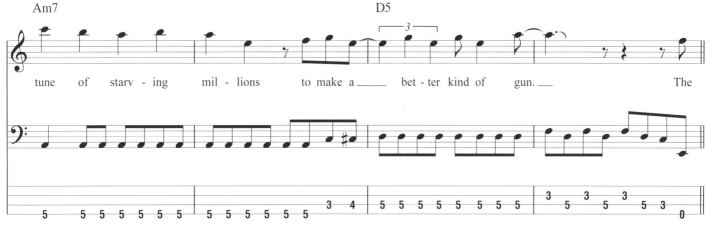

tune of starv - ing mil - lions to make a ___ bet - ter kind of gun. ___ The

Coda 2

Chorus

End half-time feel

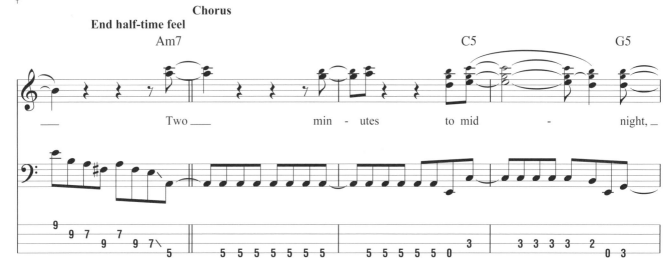

Two ___ min - utes to mid - night, ___

___ the hands ___ that threat - en ___ doom. _____

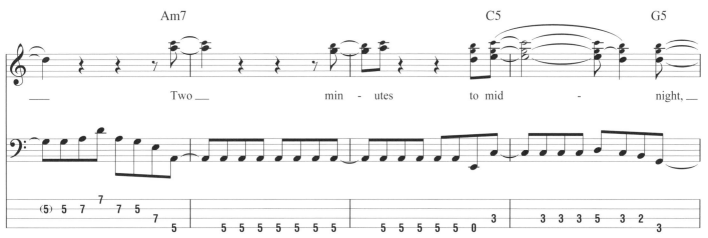

Two ___ min - utes to mid - night, ___

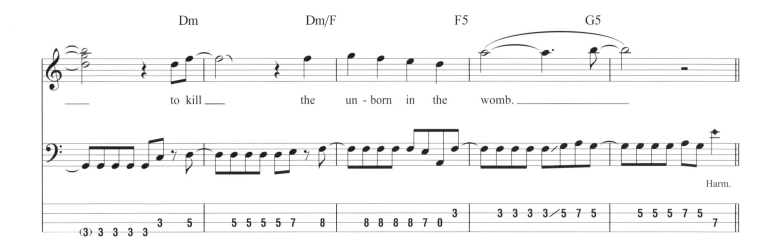

to kill ___ the un-born in the womb. _____

Outro

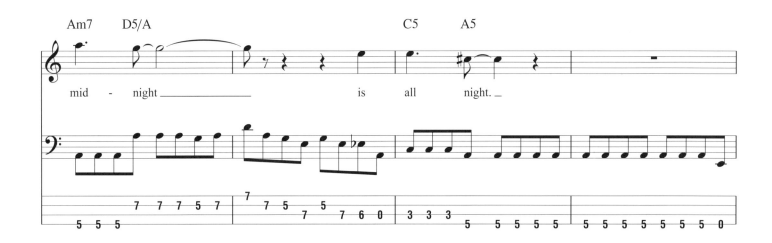

Mid - night, _____ mid - night, _____

mid - night _____ is all night. __

Mid - night, _____ mid - night, _____

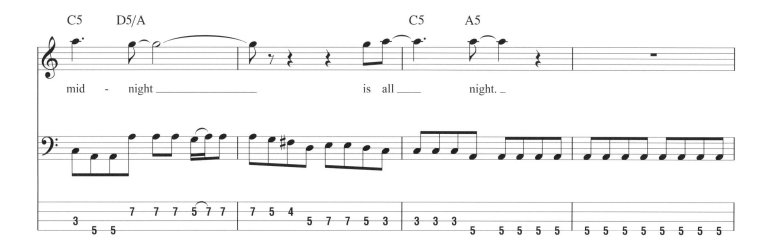

mid - night _____ is all ____ night. _

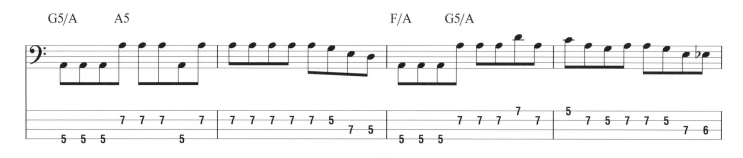

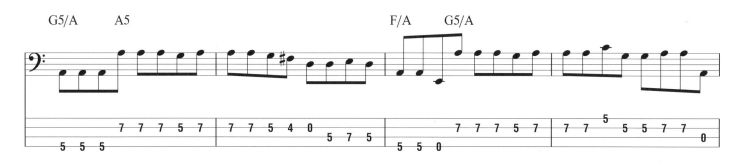

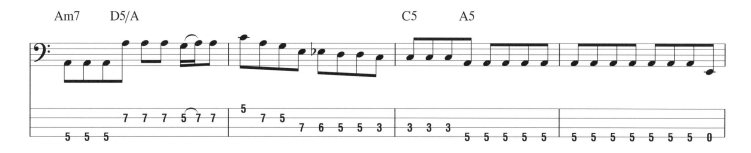

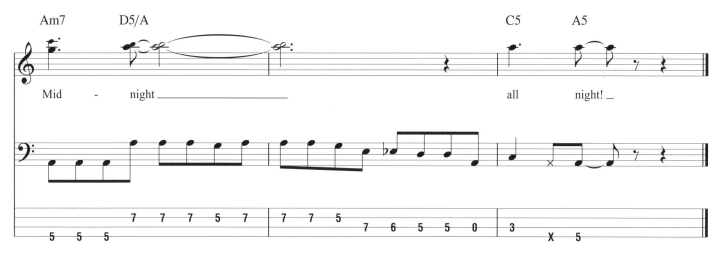

Mid - night _____ all night! _

Wasted Years

Words and Music by Adrian Smith

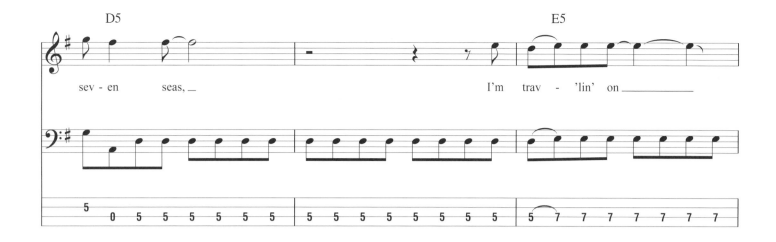

sev - en seas, ___ I'm trav - 'lin' on ___

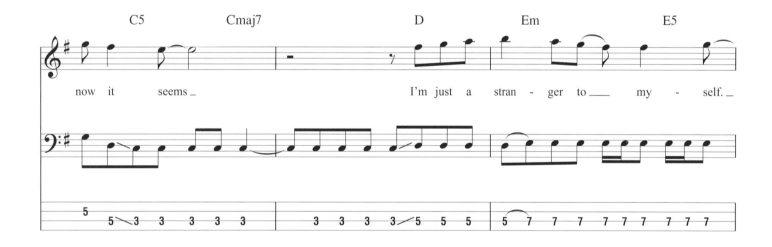

far ___ and wide. ___ But

now it seems ___ I'm just a stran - ger to ___ my - self. ___

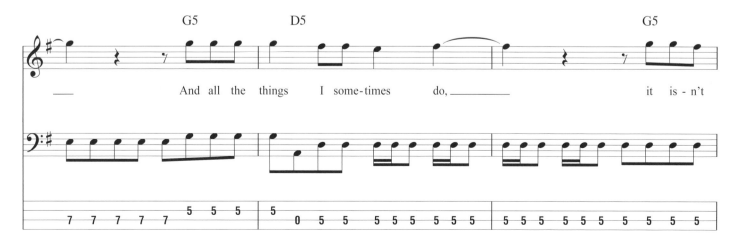

___ And all the things I some-times do, ___ it is - n't

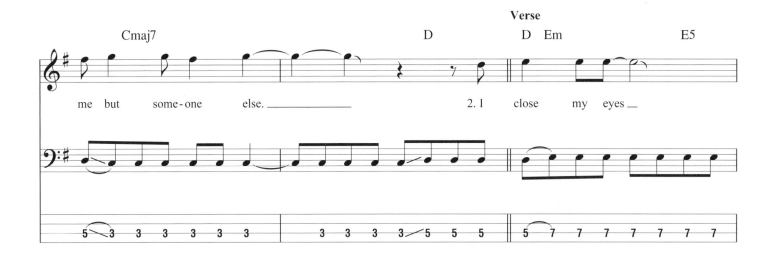

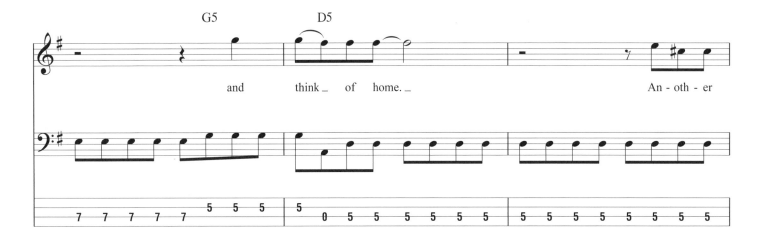

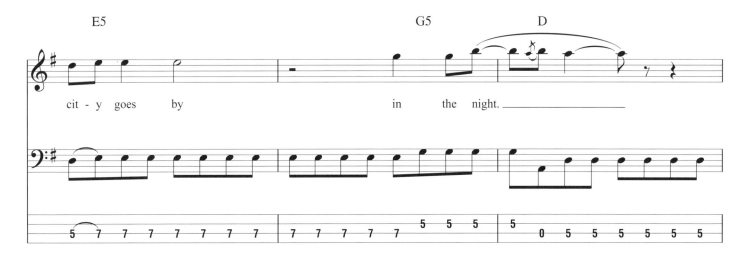

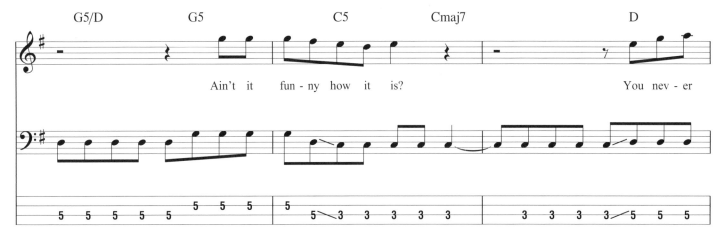

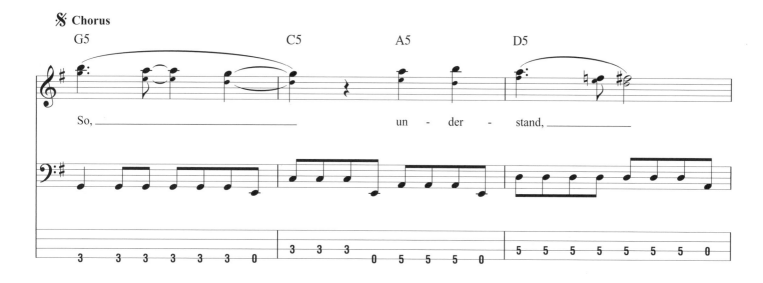

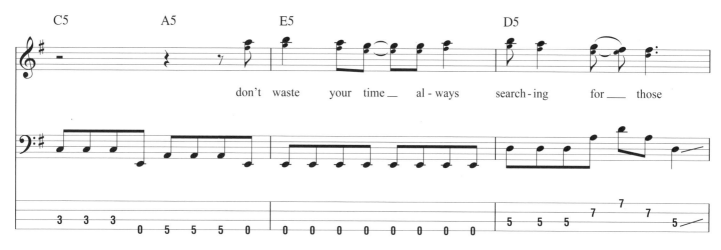

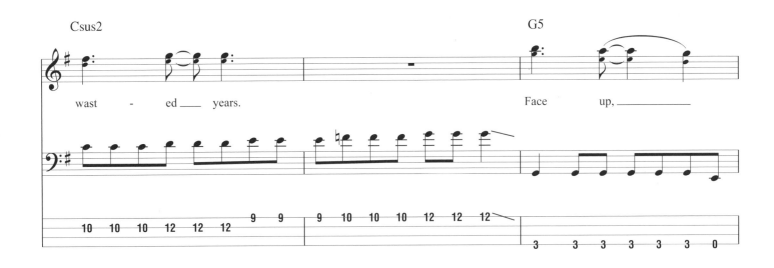

wast - ed ____ years.   Face up, ____

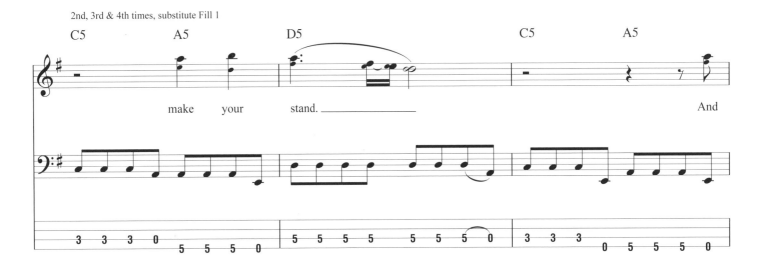

2nd, 3rd & 4th times, substitute Fill 1

make your stand. ____   And

To Coda 2 ⊕

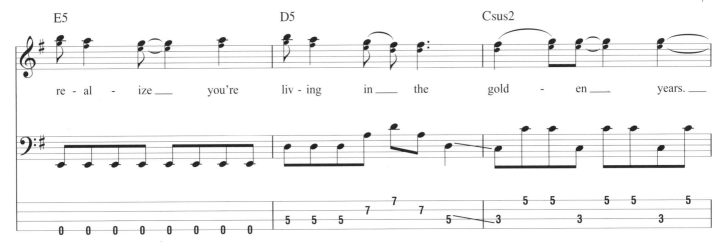

re - al - ize ____ you're liv - ing in ____ the gold - en ____ years. ____

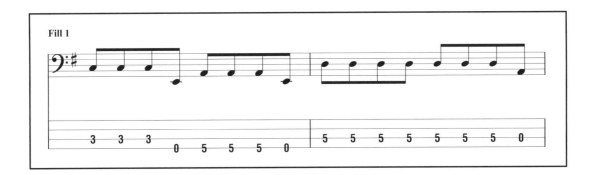

Fill 1

can't find _ the words to say, _ it's hard to make it through an - oth - er day. _

_ And it makes me want to cry and throw my

D.S. al Coda 1

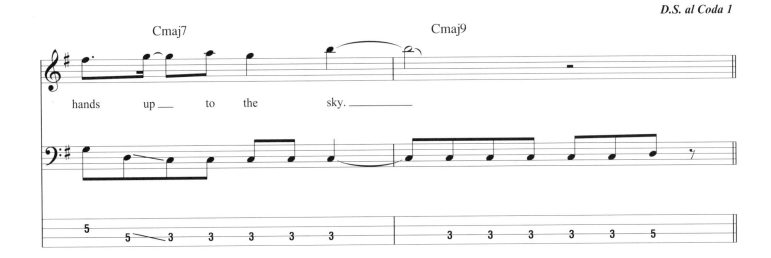

hands up _ to the sky. _

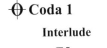

Coda 1

Interlude

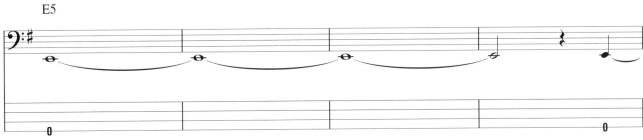

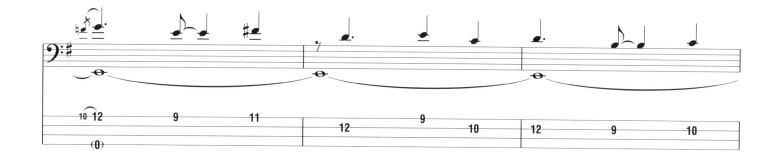

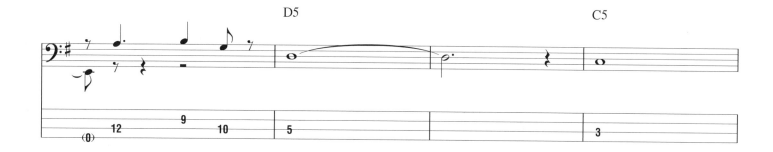

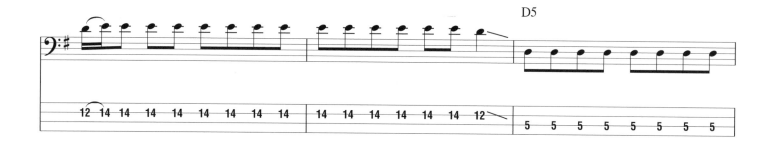

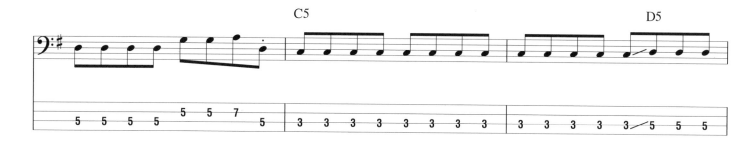

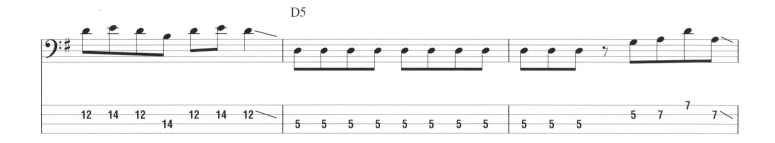

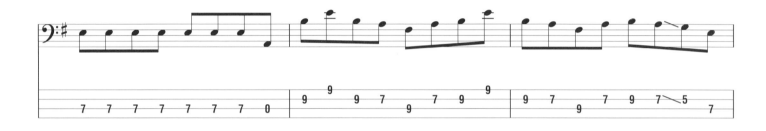

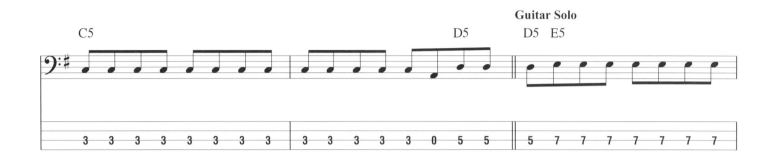

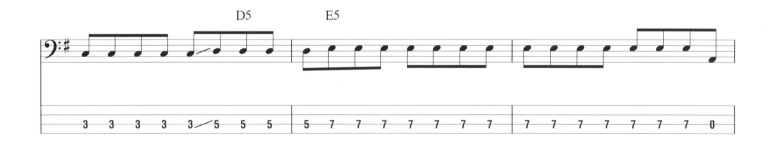

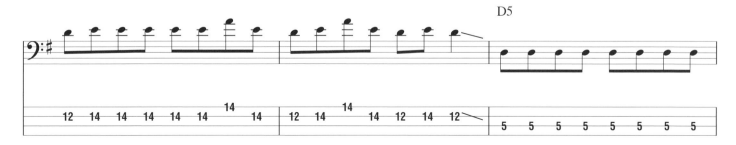

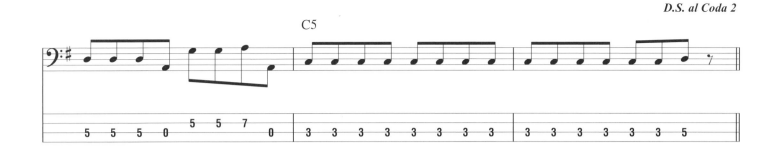

C5

◊ Coda 2   *D.S. al Coda 3*   **◊ Coda 3**

Outro

E5

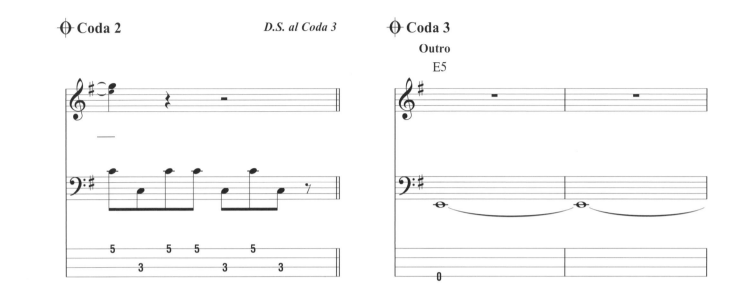

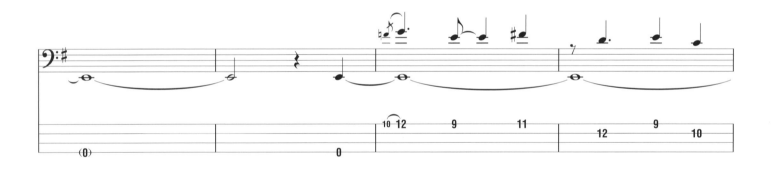

D5

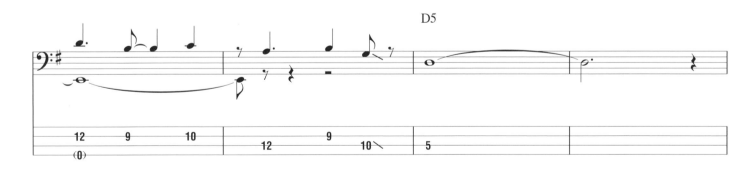

C   G/B   Am   G   A5 G5 E5

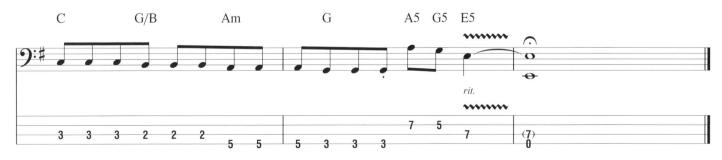

rit.

Hal•Leonard® BASS PLAY-ALONG

The Bass Play-Along™ Series will help you play your favorite songs quickly and easily! Just follow the tab, listen to the audio to hear how the bass should sound, and then play-along using the separate backing tracks. The melody and lyrics are also included in the book in case you want to sing, or to simply help you follow along. The audio files are enhanced so you can adjust the recording to any tempo without changing pitch!

1. Rock
00699674 Book/Online Audio $16.99

2. R&B
00699675 Book/Online Audio $16.99

3. Songs for Beginners
00346426 Book/Online Audio $16.99

4. '90s Rock
00294992 Book/Online Audio $16.99

5. Funk
00699680 Book/Online Audio $16.99

6. Classic Rock
00699678 Book/Online Audio $17.99

8. Punk Rock
00699813 Book/CD Pack $12.95

9. Blues
00699817 Book/Online Audio $16.99

10. Jimi Hendrix – Smash Hits
00699815 Book/Online Audio $17.99

11. Country
00699818 Book/CD Pack $12.95

12. Punk Classics
00699814 Book/CD Pack $12.99

13. The Beatles
00275504 Book/Online Audio $17.99

14. Modern Rock
00699821 Book/CD Pack $14.99

15. Mainstream Rock
00699822 Book/CD Pack $14.99

16. '80s Metal
00699825 Book/CD Pack $16.99

17. Pop Metal
00699826 Book/CD Pack $14.99

18. Blues Rock
00699828 Book/CD Pack $19.99

19. Steely Dan
00700203 Book/Online Audio $17.99

20. The Police
00700270 Book/Online Audio $19.99

21. Metallica: 1983-1988
00234338 Book/Online Audio $19.99

22. Metallica: 1991-2016
00234339 Book/Online Audio $19.99

23. Pink Floyd –
Dark Side of The Moon
00700847 Book/Online Audio $16.99

24. Weezer
00700960 Book/CD Pack $17.99

25. Nirvana
00701047 Book/Online Audio $17.99

26. Black Sabbath
00701180 Book/Online Audio $17.99

27. Kiss
00701181 Book/Online Audio $17.99

28. The Who
00701182 Book/Online Audio $19.99

29. Eric Clapton
00701183 Book/Online Audio $17.99

30. Early Rock
00701184 Book/CD Pack $15.99

31. The 1970s
00701185 Book/CD Pack $14.99

32. Cover Band Hits
00211598 Book/Online Audio $16.99

33. Christmas Hits
00701197 Book/CD Pack $12.99

34. Easy Songs
00701480 Book/Online Audio $17.99

35. Bob Marley
00701702 Book/Online Audio $17.99

36. Aerosmith
00701886 Book/CD Pack $14.99

37. Modern Worship
00701920 Book/Online Audio $19.99

38. Avenged Sevenfold
00702386 Book/CD Pack $16.99

39. Queen
00702387 Book/Online Audio $17.99

40. AC/DC
14041594 Book/Online Audio $17.99

41. U2
00702582 Book/Online Audio $19.99

42. Red Hot Chili Peppers
00702991 Book/Online Audio $19.99

43. Paul McCartney
00703079 Book/Online Audio $19.99

44. Megadeth
00703080 Book/CD Pack $16.99

45. Slipknot
00703201 Book/CD Pack $17.99

46. Best Bass Lines Ever
00103359 Book/Online Audio $19.99

47. Dream Theater
00111940 Book/Online Audio $24.99

48. James Brown
00117421 Book/CD Pack $16.99

49. Eagles
00119936 Book/Online Audio $17.99

50. Jaco Pastorius
00128407 Book/Online Audio $17.99

51. Stevie Ray Vaughan
00146154 Book/CD Pack $16.99

52. Cream
00146159 Book/Online Audio $19.99

56. Bob Seger
00275503 Book/Online Audio $16.99

57. Iron Maiden
00278398 Book/Online Audio $17.99

58. Southern Rock
00278436 Book/Online Audio $17.99

HAL•LEONARD®

Prices, contents, and availability subject to change without notice.

Visit Hal Leonard Online at **www.halleonard.com**

BASS RECORDED VERSIONS

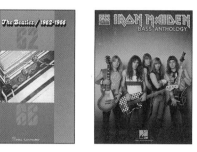

Bass Recorded Versions feature authentic transcriptions written in standard notation and tablature for bass guitar. This series features complete bass lines from the classics to contemporary superstars.

25 Essential Rock Bass Classics
00690210 / $19.99

Avenged Sevenfold – Nightmare
00691054 / $19.99

The Beatles – Abbey Road
00128336 / $24.99

The Beatles – 1962-1966
00690556 / $19.99

The Beatles – 1967-1970
00690557 / $24.99

Best of Bass Tab
00141806 / $17.99

The Best of Blink 182
00690549 / $18.99

Blues Bass Classics
00690291 / $22.99

Boston – Bass Collection
00690935 / $19.95

Stanley Clarke – Collection
00672307 / $22.99

Dream Theater – Bass Anthology
00119345 / $29.99

Funk Bass Bible
00690744 / $27.99

Hard Rock Bass Bible
00690746 / $22.99

**Jimi Hendrix –
Are You Experienced?**
00690371 / $17.95

Jimi Hendrix – Bass Tab Collection
00160505 / $24.99

Iron Maiden – Bass Anthology
00690867 / $24.99

Jazz Bass Classics
00102070 / $19.99

The Best of Kiss
00690080 / $22.99

**Lynyrd Skynyrd –
All-Time Greatest Hits**
00690956 / $24.99

Bob Marley – Bass Collection
00690568 / $24.99

Mastodon – Crack the Skye
00691007 / $19.99

Megadeth – Bass Anthology
00691191 / $22.99

Metal Bass Tabs
00103358 / $22.99

Best of Marcus Miller
00690811 / $29.99

Motown Bass Classics
00690253 / $19.99

Muse – Bass Tab Collection
00123275 / $22.99

Nirvana – Bass Collection
00690066 / $19.99

**Nothing More –
Guitar & Bass Collection**
00265439 / $24.99

The Offspring – Greatest Hits
00690809 / $17.95

The Essential Jaco Pastorius
00690420 / $22.99

**Jaco Pastorius –
Greatest Jazz Fusion Bass Player**
00690421 / $24.99

Pearl Jam – Ten
00694882 / $22.99

Pink Floyd – Dark Side of the Moon
00660172 / $19.99

The Best of Police
00660207 / $24.99

Pop/Rock Bass Bible
00690747 / $24.99

Queen – The Bass Collection
00690065 / $22.99

R&B Bass Bible
00690745 / $24.99

Rage Against the Machine
00690248 / $22.99

**Red Hot Chili Peppers –
BloodSugarSexMagik**
00690064 / $22.99

**Red Hot Chili Peppers –
By the Way**
00690585 / $24.99

**Red Hot Chili Peppers –
Californication**
00690390 / $22.99

**Red Hot Chili Peppers –
Greatest Hits**
00690675 / $22.99

**Red Hot Chili Peppers –
I'm with You**
00691167 / $22.99

**Red Hot Chili Peppers –
One Hot Minute**
00690091 / $22.99

**Red Hot Chili Peppers –
Stadium Arcadium**
00690853 / Book Only $24.95

Rock Bass Bible
00690446 / $22.99

Rolling Stones – Bass Collection
00690256 / $24.99

Royal Blood
00151826 / $24.99

**Rush – The Spirit of Radio:
Greatest Hits 1974-1987**
00323856 / $24.99

Best of Billy Sheehan
00173972 / $24.99

Slap Bass Bible
00159716 / $29.99

Sly & The Family Stone for Bass
00109733 / $24.99

Best of Yes
00103044 / $24.99

Best of ZZ Top for Bass
00691069 / $24.99

Visit Hal Leonard Online at
www.halleonard.com

Prices, contents & availability subject to change without notice.
Some products may not be available outside the U.S.A.

BUILD UP YOUR BASS CHOPS

100 FUNK/R&B LESSONS

Expand your bass knowledge with the Bass Lesson Goldmine series! Featuring 100 individual modules covering a giant array of topics, each lesson in this Funk/R&B volume includes detailed instruction with playing examples presented in standard notation and tablature. You'll also get extremely useful tips, scale diagrams, chord grids, photos, and more to reinforce your learning experience plus audio tracks featuring performance demos of all the examples in the book!

00131463 Book/Online Audio $24.99

BASS AEROBICS

by Jon Liebman

A 52-week, one-exercise-per-week workout program for developing, improving, and maintaining bass guitar technique. This book/CD will benefit all levels of players, from beginners to advanced, in all musical styles. The CD includes demos as well as play-along grooves. By using this program you'll increase your speed, improve your dexterity and accuracy, heighten your coordination, and increase your groove vocabulary!

00696437 Book/Online Audio $19.99

BASS FRETBOARD ATLAS

by Joe Charupakorn

Mastering the bass neck has always been a challenge, even for very experienced players. The diagrams in *Bass Fretboard Atlas* will help you quickly memorize scales and arpeggios that may have previously seemed impossible to grasp. You'll be able to easily see and understand how scale and arpeggio shapes are laid out and how they connect and overlap across the neck.

00201827 .... $19.99

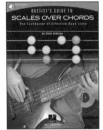

BASSIST'S GUIDE TO SCALES OVER CHORDS

by Chad Johnson

With *Bassist's Guide to Scales Over Chords*, you'll learn how these two topics are intertwined in a logical and fundamental manner. This key concept is paramount in learning how to create and improvise functional and memorable bass lines or solos reliably time and again. This book includes 136 audio tracks and 17 extended backing tracks for download or streaming online.

00151930 Book/Online Audio $19.99

FRETBOARD ROADMAPS – BASS

by Fred Sokolow & Tim Emmons

This book/audio pack will get you playing bass lines anywhere on the fretboard, in any key. You'll learn to build bass lines under chord progressions; major, minor, and pentatonic scale patterns; and much more through easy-to-follow diagrams and instructions for beginning, intermediate, and advanced players. The online audio includes 64 demonstration and play-along tracks.

00695840 Book/Online Audio $17.99

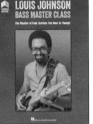

LOUIS JOHNSON – BASS MASTER CLASS

For the first time, the legendary Louis Johnson "Star Licks" bass instruction videos are being made available in book format with online access to all the classic video footage. This package compiles Volumes I and II of the original Star Licks Master Classes into one bundle, giving you over an hour and a half of instruction, while the book contains transcriptions of every example played! All music is written in both standard notation and tab.

00156138 Book with Online Video $19.99

MUSIC THEORY FOR BASS PLAYERS

by Steve Gorenberg

With this comprehensive workbook, you'll expand your fretboard knowledge and gain the freedom and confidence needed to tackle any musical challenge. Features hundreds of examples to study and practice, including loads of "real world" bass lines and play-along audio tracks to jam to! Includes over 200 demonstration and play-along audio tracks and three bass fretboard theory video lessons online for download or streaming.

00197904 Book/Online Media $24.99

JACO PASTORIUS – BASS SIGNATURE LICKS

by Dan Towey

Learn the trademark grooves and solos of the man who revolutionized bass guitar. This book/CD pack will help you take a closer look at Jaco's rich body of work through the structural, theoretical, and harmonic analysis of these classic recordings: Birdland • Bright Size Life • Come On, Come Over • Continuum • Donna Lee • God Must Be a Boogie Man • Kuru • Liberty City • Night Passage • Palladium • Port of Entry • Portrait of Tracy • Rockin' in Rhythm • Talk to Me • Teen Town.

00695544 Book/CD Pack $24.95

PLAY LIKE JACO PASTORIUS

THE ULTIMATE BASS LESSON

by Jon Liebman

Study the trademark songs, licks, tones and techniques of the world's greatest jazz fusion bassist, Jaco Pastorius. This comprehensive book/audio teaching method provides detailed analysis of Pastoruis' gear, techniques, styles, songs, riffs and more. Each book comes with a unique code that will give you access to audio files of all the music in the book online. This pack looks at 15 of Jaco's most influential songs.

00128409 Book/Online Audio $19.99

STUFF! GOOD BASS PLAYERS SHOULD KNOW

by Glenn Letsch

Provides valuable tips on performing, recording, the music business, instruments and equipment (including electronics), grooves, fills, soloing techniques, care & maintenance, and more. Covers rock, jazz, blues, R&B and funk through demos of authentic grooves. The accompanying recordings include many of the examples in the book performed both in solo bass format and in a full-band setting so you can hear how important concepts fit in with other instruments and ensembles.

00696014 Book/Online Audio $19.99

WARM-UP EXERCISES FOR BASS GUITAR

by Steve Gorenberg

Bass players: customize your warm-up routine with this fantastic collection of stretches, coordination exercises, pentatonic scales, major and minor scales, and arpeggios sure to limber up your fingers and hands and get you ready to play in top form!

00148760 .... $9.99

HAL•LEONARD®

www.halleonard.com

View our website for hundreds more bass books!

Prices, contents, and availability subject to change without notice.